SEA STORIES

of the Inside Passage

Sea Stories

of the

INSIDE PASSAGE

In the Wake of the Nid

text and illustrations by
Iain Lawrence

Foreword by Anne Vipond

Fine Edge
Productions

Visit our internet web site for our latest products or to download our supplements:

http://www.fineedge.com

Cover photograph by Réanne Hemingway-Douglass

Book design by Melanie Haage

Printed in the United States of America

Library of Congress Cataloging-in-Publication Data

Lawrence, Iain, 1955–

    Sea stories of the Inside Passage : in the wake of the Nid / Iain Lawrence.

      p. cm.

    ISBN 0-938665-47-2

    1. Inside Passage—Description and travel—Anecdotes.

2. Seafaring life—Inside Passage—Anecdotes.   3. Lawrence, Iain,

    1955–   —Journeys—Inside Passage—Anecdotes.   I. Title

F1089.I5L39   1997   97-283

917.9804'5—dc21   CIP

For Kristin

About the Author

Iain Lawrence was born in Sault Ste. Marie, Ontario and has lived in British Columbia since 1975. As a child of nine, he was taught to sail on a small lake on the prairies. Before becoming a full-time writer, he worked as a salmon fisherman and a journalist. He practices many of the traditional maritime arts, including building ships in bottles and carving scrimshaw on modern materials. Iain currently lives at a remote radio-transmission site on Digby Island on the North Coast of British Columbia with quilter/writer Kristin Miller and a dog named Skipper.

"We are caretakers of a place without roads, only a dock below the house and a helicopter pad in the front yard. Every summer, we go sailing, travelling farther as our boats grow bigger. We started with a 20-foot cutter and moved up to a naval whaleboat called *Nid.* Recently we bought *Connection,* a 32-foot ocean cruiser built by Kristin's brother."

Iain continues to write a newspaper feature column about his and Kristin's sailing experiences. Out of their voyages came *Sea Stories of the Inside Passage,* and *Far-Away Places,* a narrative guide published in 1995. His first novel, a sea story for young adults is scheduled for publication in 1998.

contents

Acknowledgements

A large number of people helped in one way or another with the creation of this book. Seven years ago, Les Yates invited me to write a column for his new community paper, *Prince Rupert This Week,* where original versions of these stories have appeared. Among its staff who offered constant encouragement are Bruce Wishart, Gerry Dieter, Paul Anderson, and Yvonne Simmons. Several of the stories have also appeared in *Pacific Yachting Magazine* and for that I owe my thanks to John Shinnick and his successor Duart Snow. But the stories would still be a scattered collection of paper and computer files if it were not for Don and Réanne Douglass of Fine Edge Productions. They spent many, many hours sorting and editing, reading and re-reading and the result is as much their work as mine. To my parents, as always, I owe thanks for their help and support, their care, and their love. My thanks go to Kristin for making voyaging a pleasure, and also to everyone we've met along the coast, all whose stories are told here.

—*Iain Lawrence*

Foreword
by Anne Vipond

There are many beautiful coastlines in the world but there is only one Inside Passage. Stretching more than a thousand nautical miles, from Washington State's Puget Sound in the south to Alaska's Glacier Bay in the north, this famous waterway both inspires and challenges mariners with its deep fjords, twisting channels and racing tidal currents. Those who pilot these intricate waters usually head home with a good yarn or two, and some of the best are shared with us in this new compilation of stories and illustrations by Canadian writer and yachtsman Iain Lawrence.

The Canadian portion of the Inside Passage, especially the remote anchorages between Cape Caution and Dixon Entrance, has long been one of my favorite cruising areas. Far removed from the cities of the south, this northern region of steep-sided channels and hanging falls is largely untouched by human development. Red-roofed lighthouses, painted white, dot the route made famous by the Klondike Gold Rush but their presence is overshadowed by snowcapped mountains and the sheer number of forested islands past which the water weaves.

This scenic stretch of coastline represents home waters to Lawrence and he captures its unique texture in stories told with wit, charm and nuggets of insight. When he and Kristen Miller take to the water in their vessel *Nid,* the reader gets to join them on their seafaring adventures, sharing their moments of terror and tranquility as they discover new things about sailing and about themselves.

Many a mariner dreams of one day cruising the Inside Passage and experiencing firsthand its grandeur. Meanwhile, reading Lawrence's *Sea Stories of the Inside Passage* is the next best thing to cruising these waters in your own boat.

Anne, the author of *Alaska By Cruise Ship,* and her husband William Kelly are regular contributors to *Pacific Yachting* magazine. Their articles are based on numerous voyages they have made along the Inside Passage in their 35-foot sailboat, *Sway*

North to Alaska

So you're heading up the Inside Passage, north to Alaska! The phrase has the same ring to it, the same calling of lonesome adventure, that it did a century ago when the gold seekers stormed up these channels on their way to the Klondike or Nome.

They left from the docks of Seattle, from Victoria and Vancouver, in schooners and sternwheelers, in sailboats and steamships, cramming aboard any craft that could float. And north they went, in a stream, up the sheltered channels that were all these boats could cope with.

Why, it sounds a lot like today.

The Inside Passage is a watery highway travelled by everything from inflatable kayaks to cruise ships that look, as they glide past in the night, like skyscrapers lying on their side.

In Bella Bella we met a couple in a boat like a nutshell, a tiny thing, but they'd sailed up from Port Hardy, anchoring each night with a bungee cord. They'd rounded Cape Caution enveloped in fog, with a big powerboat creeping along in their wake, full of men from the prairies, lost on the ocean.

Along the Inside Passage, you'll travel through drowned canyons where the bottom's farther away than either shore. You see mountains forever in snow, and forests that start at the edge of the water and stretch all the way to the Rockies. You see eagles and bears, and eagles and whales, and eagles until you can't bother looking. And when the day is done, your problem isn't finding an anchorage; it's choosing between them.

But don't let the name mislead you; it's not entirely an "inside" passage. When the westerlies blow in Queen Charlotte Sound, the swells can look like mountains. A friend still talks of the day he sailed over a crest to see a troller hidden in the trough below him, poles and all.

In Dixon Entrance we found holes in the sea, gaping pits among the waves, and we sailed over their edge and dropped to the bottom, ringed all around by water. We've crossed Milbanke Sound in a snowstorm—in June—with the waves bursting like cannon shots on every shore. The Strait of Georgia, Queen Charlotte Strait, Fitz Hugh Sound and Chatham Sound: they are all miserable bits of water when the wind blows like a Fury.

For most of its length, the passage is much the same as those gold seekers saw it. But the men and women who rushed to Alaska a hundred years ago changed the land they passed through. Dozens of aids to navigation were established to guide them on their way, and it was Klondike gold that built much of Port Essington and parts of Prince Rupert, and places that are no longer here. And if there are more people now on the Inside Passage, they live in fewer places. Gone are the cannery towns, the fishing villages, the homesteads by the sea. You can still see the remains of those settlements, the tumbled-down houses and overgrown dikes.

You can also see the signs of a civilization that dates back thousands of years—fish traps and middens, and beaches cleared for canoes. If you know where to look, you might even find totems, wooden creatures hiding in the bush; or stumble on tidy patches of devil's club, square at the edges—the ghostly outline of a longhouse, where the forest won't grow.

You're going north to Alaska! You'll have a wonderful time.

A Manner of Speaking

IT ALL STARTED ON A WINDY DAY ON THE CENTRAL COAST, our first voyage together on the *Nid*. We bowled down Fitz Hugh Sound, Kristin happy to steer with nothing to hit and no worries of gybing. The boat was rolling along, a hum in the rigging and a chorus of creaks and groans from the hull, like a shanty sung by a tired old sailor. It was a wonderful day.

"Ease the mainsheet," I said to Kristin at the tiller. "Let her fall off a bit."

She stared at me. "What?"

"Fall off," I said. But it might have come out "FALL OFF!!" for she glared at me in that pre-dawn darkness of near anger.

"And can you tell me what that means?" she said. "In English?"

"Just exactly that," I said, a bit impatiently maybe. I waved my hands through the air as though it would help her understand. "Let the sail out a bit, and turn to your left." And, yes, I suppose I sighed as well.

And then we got mad at each other. Kristin said I was babbling in a foreign language. She said I was using terms that went out with the sailing masters. "It's pretentious," she said.

And I said the words were important, that each one took the place of whole sentences. "Whole paragraphs of *English*," I think I added, italicizing the word with sarcasm. "And you should know them."

Kristin scowled. "Why?"

"I'll show you why," I said. And with a little scream, I picked up my life-jacket and hurled it over the side. "There," I said. "I've fallen overboard."

"That's really stupid," she said. Then she leaned on the tiller, and the boat slewed round across the wind. "What should I do?"

"Don't ask me," I said. "I'm drowning out there."

I sat in the companionway, below the boom as it crashed back and forth and watched her wrestling with the sheets and the sails and the tiller. I might have been laughing, but I don't like to think about that now.

"Well," Kristin snapped. "I could do this all day and not get anywhere."

"See?" I said. "See?"

"No," she cried. "I have to learn to sail, not talk!"

And that was the end of our conversation, for a very long time. It was nearly the end of our lifejacket, too, though we did get *that* back in the end.

But the first chance she got, Kristin bought a paperback book: the Penguin *Dictionary of Sailing*. "I'll learn the words," she said, "as long as you promise not to spring new ones on me. It only cost twenty-five cents."

She read it, and studied it, and was soon talking away about luffs and clews and marline spikes. She leafed through the book and came up with words that would have sent Joseph Conrad searching through his thesaurus.

Whenever she put it down, I picked it up myself. "Do you know what a hen frigate is?" I asked

"What?"

I read from the book. "A vessel," I said, "where the . . . " I had to stop, I was laughing so hard. " . . . where the captain permits his wife to interfere with the running of the ship."

"I don't think that's very funny," she said.

And then, over dinner in the cabin, with our coats and jackets swinging on their hooks, peas rolling back and forth across the plates, Kristin wanted salt for her potatoes. She reached out her hand, shifting her knee to keep the plate level.

Her fingers were curling, beckoning. Without looking, she balanced her teacup against the roll of the boat and shifted her knee again. "Pass me Lot's wife, will you?" she growled.

I handed her the salt shaker and smiled. My God, I thought, I'd created a master.

This Is Sailing

IN THE MORNING, AS WE LAY AT ANCHOR, A FOG CAME SWIRLING IN. It was a thick, putrid fog that bubbled like sewer gas, all yellow and grey. An hour after dawn, when the wind came up, it passed through the trees in a greasy wad and the branches tore it to shreds. And it came out on our side of the narrow spit reduced to thin and ragged spider webs, transparent under a smoldering sun.

We raised the anchors and lashed them down. The sails, when we took off the covers and raised them wing-on-wing, were splotched with dampness, dappled like butterfly wings. We drifted over a sheet of silver, silent as a cloud. The moisture dried from the sailcloth in wispy curls, rose from the decks and the hatch covers and the coiled ropes, as though we were only another bit of the vanishing fog, and the whole boat might turn to steam under that burning sun.

"Now this is sailing," said Kristin, lathering sunscreen lotion on arms and naked shoulders.

A mile from shore, in a rising breeze, the sea turned from milky white to a

postcard blue. The sails filled into bulging curves and the boat, with a creak of old-woman's bones, bent to it and hauled herself along.

The first whitecaps appeared, ahead and behind, and then—like spring flowers—they sprouted everywhere and tossed their heads in the wind. The boat surged forward and burst through the waves. Each one broke in a cloud of spray, and a rainbow wreathed the bowsprit. We heeled further and further, until water flowed down the deck and lapped at the cabin side.

"Now this is sailing," I said.

Kristin scrambled through the hatchway and dogged the portholes shut. We reefed the main and brought in the staysail, and as I wrestled it down, pinned it on the deck, we hurtled sideways into a bank of writhing fog.

Our world closed to a blue-grey dome. The horizon vanished and there was no up, no down. Everything on the boat—the rain coats and towels hanging on their hooks, the ropes coiled in the rigging, even the compass—hung suspended at strange angles in the air.

"Steer 260," said Kristin, but when she tapped the compass it tilted upright in its gimbals and reeled around to 190 degrees. And we went charging through the fog with the waves roaring out of a grey nothing, and spray flying everywhere.

"Now this," said Kristin, "is just plain scary."

It's evening, and the sea is burning. Embers have been scattered on its surface, a white-hot glow; they shimmer red and yellow as the sun comes down. A huge and fiery ball, it touches the sea and it melts; it spreads like a lava flow, streaming pools of molten sun from horizon to the shore.

We sit in the cockpit, in silence, and watch the water cool to shades of violet as night settles in. Already the furled sails are wet with dew; fog will come again with darkness. We're all alone at the creation of a day.

And this—is sailing.

Respecting the Coast

WE WANTED A GOOD ANCHORAGE, a hurricane hole. Before the next dawn came, the winds would reach sixty knots. I remember it well, the care we took selecting a little bight off the Inside Passage, the trepidation as we settled in for the night with two anchors down and sixty pounds of lead suspended on the rode. I sat up until midnight, until the rain came sweeping over the deck like a drummer's marching band.

The first gusts of wind came moaning through the trees. Ropes stretched like drawn springs. They creaked and snapped on the mooring bitt. Twice I went out in the rain before I could go to bed knowing the boat would look after herself.

It wasn't yet dawn when the wind woke us, stronger than ever we'd heard. It whistled and shrieked in the rigging, then rose again, and the sound became a dismal moan. We heard waves slapping on the hull, felt the tug of the anchors at the bow, and when we looked out, at first light, low clouds were scudding past like great black tumble-weeds rolling across the sky.

I remember thinking how glad I was that we weren't "out there." The boat was sailing on her anchors, laying herself sideways in the gusts. But we were still in the same spot; we were luckier than some.

A hundred miles away, a boat capsized that night in hurricane winds and waves thirty feet high. But on the central coast, the storm battered at us and passed quickly on. By noon, the wind had all but stopped. It was sunny and warm; we could hear the surf outside pounding on the rocks. I wanted to get under way while we still had the tide behind us.

"It'll be awful out there," said Kristin.

We had a narrows to pass, and we could never buck the tide through there. "If we don't go now," I said, "we're stuck until tomorrow."

"So let's wait," she said.

I didn't want to wait, not there in so gloomy and sad a place where ruined houses lay flat in the trees, covered with garbage scattered by bears. It smelled of mud and swarmed with flies.

There was no wind at all in the anchorage. The storm had passed us by, though the sea would take a day to settle down. I said we could take the dinghy and row across the harbour. There was a little island on the other side, and we could hike across it to have a look at the sea.

"Okay," said Kristin. That sounded all right. There was no harm in looking.

On the chart, the island seemed narrow and flat. But we clambered through a tangle of wind-fallen trees, up a slope and through a valley, down a gully to the shore. The sea didn't look too bad out there, with every rock and reef whitewashed by surf, outlined in foamy streaks. As we stood at the edge of the trees, a cabin cruiser and a seine boat came churning through the narrows, the tide against them. They turned on a course that would take them inside the island, and we watched them roll in the swell. They soared up on the wave tops and vanished in the troughs, but no; it didn't look so bad out there.

"Okay," said Kristin. "We'll go."

It was harder rowing back, the tiny Avon stuffed with a dog and slickers we didn't need; Kristin and I were rolly fat and sweating in our Floater coats and foam-filled pants. "I think I was maybe being too cautious," said Kristin.

When the cabin cruiser came chugging toward us, and the engines dropped to an idle, we thought they were going to offer us a tow across the harbour. But they only passed at dead-slow speed, three people gawking at us through binoculars in a line behind the windows.

Kristin laughed. "They'll wonder what we're doing out here," she said. "You can't see our boat because it's behind the point."

Behind the cruiser came the seine boat. It was aluminum, all-over silver, and shining so brightly it threw slashes of sunlight back in our eyes. It slowed, and stopped close behind us.

"Well, that's nice," said Kristin.

A loud-hailer clicked and hummed. A voice boomed across the few feet of water. "Good morning," it said, and Kristin turned to wave. She was smiling.

The voice seemed to come from the boat itself; we could see no one at the windows. It had a tinny voice, an aluminum voice. It said, "Not too brilliant being out here on a day like this."

Kristin's head snapped back, her smile erased. I pulled on the little oars and set the dinghy going.

The seine boat didn't move. It bellowed at us through the quiet harbour. "You've got to watch this country," it said. It sounded like Robocop. "You've got to have some respect for this coast."

I remember the feeling, a mix of embarrassment and anger. But we didn't say anything back. How can you carry on a conversation with a metal boat? Over Kristin's shoulder, I saw it shudder as the propeller turned. It slid off to the south as we rowed in behind the point and was gone long before we'd made our own boat ready for the sea.

Beyond the island, there was barely enough wind to fill the jib. But the seas were big, and we slid and rolled through the swells. Little *Nid* hurled herself from crests to troughs. She buried her bowsprit in the waves, and dipped her gunwales in foaming water.

We passed through the narrows on the last of the tide, with the surf breaking on each side in white, firework-bursts. The spray glistened on the rocks and blew through the trees. We came down from watery mountains, down through watery hills, onto a desert that was flat and calm and baked by the sun. And I remember thinking how much I love this coast. How much I respect it.

"The clouds came, in dark bands with silvered edges, like scythes swung across the sea."

Growing a Ghost Town

AT OCEANIC, WE ANCHORED IN A KINDERGARTEN PAINTING. The land was a green smudge, the sky an unnatural blue. That big ball of a sun streaming starfish arms of crayon yellow cast our shadows on the deck, thin as stick men. It gave the dog stilts for legs, a blotch with head and tail.

Kristin picked up the binoculars and aimed them at the trees, at the bit of Smith Island shore, where once there'd been a village. "Not much here," she said.

Not much at all. I stood with my hand in the rigging and sighed. We'd come a long way to find this place, but it was nothing like what I'd imagined. Nothing like the ghost town of Castle.

When I was eight years old, my family drove through Montana, following old wagon roads over desert and prairie. We went where Lewis and Clark had been, where gunmen had ridden on silver-trimmed horses, and where prairie schooners had crossed a sea of grass, we followed them. At night we pulled off at the side of the road, at a creek where Dad could water the old car, and we'd sit by a fire in a cottonwood grove.

It seemed to me we were wandering, going east one day, south the next. And one day we went up a hill covered with tumbleweed and cactus, and stumbled on a ghost town.

The buildings were blackened by the sun, charred by prairie fires. The wind blew through them, and the tumbleweeds bunched against the walls, butting at the old logs as if too stupid to go around. In the windows hung rotten lace, on the walls shreds of newspaper yellow and brittle; bed frames lay twisted and broken—skeletons in the shadows.

The town was called Castle. And I believed that ghosts lived in the buildings, walked through the streets, and sat in the moonlight on their tumbled-down porches.

Ever since, I've looked for another Castle in the wilderness. That was what I'd hoped to find at Oceanic, what I'd hoped to find before at Klekane and Kynumpt, at Lawson Harbour and Lizzie Cove. The remains of canneries and settlements are scattered through the channels of the northern coast like raisins in a bran-flakes box. They're shown on the charts—marked "Abandoned" or "Ruins"—with neat little squares drawn for the buildings.

Maybe those squares mislead me. I remember the streets and cabins of Castle and, when I find instead forests and flattened wads of buildings, I'm always disappointed .

At Oceanic, we paddled across the painted sea and landed the dinghy at the mouth of a creek. Seventy years earlier, we would have been right under the cannery, in a hiss of steam and a stench of smoke, with the Iron Chink clanking above us, gloating over its success in replacing a whole crew of Chinese workers. Now there were trees, just bushes and trees.

It had been an enormous cannery, a whole town for hundreds of people. The plant had stood three storeys high on a wharf built for steamships. There were homes and offices, work sheds and cook shacks; there were bunkhouses, net lofts and stores.

We walked up the creek where the boardwalk once was and stood in a forest where chipmunks chattered and little birds pecked at the huckleberries.

Seventy years ago, the town was filled with people everywhere, in boots and overalls; people trundling by with wooden-wheeled carts, people hurrying to the Saturday dance or staggering to Sunday service; people feeding huge gillnets into vats of poisonous blue dye and watching for boats from the Horn and Wilson Bar, from the tide rips of the Glory Hole.

In Castle, the ghosts stroll home from the mines with shovels on their shoulders, tramping over hills of cactus and sage. At Oceanic, they come in leaky old boats, pulling oars that thump and creak. On the falling tide, their skiffs spill out through Hell's Gate Slough like tossed dice, a fleet of them racing for the dock.

We walked up the stream, past squirrel middens piled at the base of trees. Deep in the woods, we found the remains of Oceanic.

This was where the houses had stood—the manager's was first, and bigger than all the rest; his assistant's next door just a bit smaller; the houses shrank in size according to the ranks of the workers, like wooden dolls that nest one inside another. The women had coaxed roses from the mud and the moss; the children had sent metal hoops rumbling down the boardwalk; the men had sat smoking pipes on the stoops at sunset. All that was gone.

We found a bit of boardwalk, a crumpled old shack. Everything else had fallen away or burned to the ground.

The creek water trickled over a bed of stones. It flowed round little triangles and octagons of broken china, shards of yellow and blue, sweeping them up and pooling them in the curve of a metal ring, like scrapings from a crematorium.

The bones of a bear lay on the beach, scattered from forest to sea. I thought it strange that his grandfathers had lived on the waste of the cannery, on garbage and fish.

It wasn't so long ago that this bit of land once hummed and throbbed. And a part of that lingered, somehow, in the cedars and the alders, in these trees that had fed on the ashes of Oceanic. Like drinking straws, their roots had sucked up the old planks, the spilled offal, the spittle of the fishermen, preserving it all in sap and wood, growing a ghost town, north-coast style.

Chasing Rainbows

A T 51°10' N, CAPE CAUTION POKES A BLUNT THUMB into the edge of the Pacific. It's the dividing point between the North Coast and the south coast: a physical barrier that boats pass with care and respect; a bureaucratic border where one pilot book stops and another begins. On one side is the warmth and sun of the south, on the other the cold and rain-sodden north.

Each year we go south, chasing rainbows down the coast. And we reach the end of them beyond the Cape, hundreds of miles and a month from home, where the islands of Queen Charlotte Strait shimmer in the sun like pots of gold.

There we stay as long as we can, until the rains come to the top end of Vancouver Island, and the first of the late-summer gales drives us back past the Cape, home from the south to the north.

But one year the rain and the gales were late in coming. Along the North Coast of the Island, the trees were withered to grey and gold, like dust-covered shrubs. It hadn't rained at all for nearly a month.

At God's Pocket, the owners of the little resort were asking their customers to conserve water. They had stopped providing showers and laundry for visiting boats, and the last of their supply came dripping out of the bathroom faucet one tiny, yellow drop at a time. "We need rain," said a sign on the door of the coffee shop.

In Port Hardy, in what should have been a normal monsoon season, the streets were hot and dusty. Dogs walked with their tongues scraping the sidewalk, and at one house lawn sprinklers hissed in the garden.

"I didn't think they'd even heard of lawn sprinklers in Port Hardy," Kristin said, and shrugged. "I'll bet the hardware salesman lives in that house."

Every day was the same. A hot wind from the west, bright sunshine and high, cotton-ball clouds. We waited for a change, prowling back and forth along the coastline like a guard dog pacing a fence. I didn't want to go. I could have stayed there forever, in a land of treasure islands, the place where the rainbows end. I always hate the day we have to head home, north to Prince Rupert, but we were down to our last five gallons of water—brown and salty, dipped from the barest trickle of a stream—so we we decided we'd better go home.

The wind backed to the southeast then, and we steered north into the morning fog. It thickened and thinned, turning from white to grey to icy blue.

And when it lifted at noon there were killer whales all around us, and Pine Island was straight ahead. By the time we reached Cape Caution, the clouds were gathering behind. And when Egg Island slipped astern, the wind was crisp and cold, and the clouds were swooping low, weeping distant rain.

We skirted Dugout Rocks in gusts of wind that sent the waves tumbling past in roaring foam. The rain hit us then, the North Coast rain, so heavy it bounced off the sea, flattening the waves to pocked sheets like plates of hammered copper. We set a bucket against the mast, at the foot of the sail, and filled it twice from the drips that streamed along the boom.

We put on layers of rain gear, dragging coats and gloves out from the bottom of bins stuffed with canned corn and kidney beans, bins we hadn't opened in a very long time. We huddled down with the wind at our backs, driving north, a ghost ship in the swirling mist. Driving north, a wild woman in long skirts and blowing scarves, ragged in the gale.

The sails snapped and shook, flinging off silver beads of water, and Cape Calvert flashed by, a dim shadow in the clouds. I touched Kristin on the shoulder. My hands were white, the fingers as puffy as cauliflowers.

"We're back on the North Coast," I said.

She looked up, water dribbling from the peak of her hood, a little rivulet streaming from her collar. "Yes. Nice to be back, isn't it?"

Then we were inside, in the lee of Calvert Island, and the sun came out. It was just a pale glow at first, then a bright ball perched on the shoulder of Entry Cone. As we turned into Safety Cove, a rainbow arched beside us, bright and perfect as a stained-glass ornament, so close it seemed to settle in the rigging.

I stared at it, and tried to touch it, and it seemed that I could move my hand right through the bars of light. I tapped Kristin on the shoulder again, so she would see it too. I was afraid that she'd look, and frown, and say it wasn't there at all, because I'd never seen a rainbow like that before. I touched my eyes, thinking it might have formed somehow on the beads of water on my lashes.

She was scowling when she looked up, her eyes nearly squinted shut. Then her face brightened, and a square of sunlight slid across her cheek. The rainbow glowed beside us.

"It's sitting in the cockpit here," she said. And she stood up, to see it better.

"The gold's in the boat," she said. "The treasure's right here. It means we don't have to look any farther than this."

The Orphan

I WENT TO SEE WHAT THE TIDE HAD WASHED IN, and around the point from the village I came across a body, a tiny little body. It lay up among the driftwood logs, on a patch of seaweed, and I thought at first it must be a cat, the pale hump of a drowned cat.

I stepped closer. Then it stretched, and rolled from its belly to its side. It was asleep, and in whatever dream it dreamt, its mouth moved as though suckling.

It was a baby seal, just a few days old. It heard me, I suppose, and opened eyes that were almost human in shape, but dark as molasses and twice too big for the small dome of a head. It was covered in a fur of silvery ash and cried out in a pathetic croak of a voice, a sad little mewling that sounded just like "mama."

I didn't know what to do. I looked at it and wondered, and suddenly saw a sign on the beach, so obvious I didn't know how I'd missed it. On a piece of cardboard propped against a log, someone had written, "Please do not disturb."

For a day and a night and a whole, long morning, the baby had lain there in a manger of sorts that someone had made from logs padded with seaweed. And the village had watched over it, helping it, hoping the mother would come and take it away.

That looked doubtful, though. It wasn't a place where seals liked to go. The beach was stone and gravelly sand, and scuff marks showed how the baby had crawled back and forth, dragging itself on sad little flippers. Calling out in that lonely voice.

Last summer we'd heard the same thing. "Mama. Maa-maaa." In the evening, anchored in a bay surrounded by islands of rock and trees, we had listened to it with sadness and yearning. In the morning, we saw the baby seal lying on a ledge, just a foot from the water. It couldn't possibly have dragged

itself farther than that. But that baby's mother was never more than a moment away. Most of the time she lay right against her baby, one flipper curled like an arm across the little white mound. When she saw us, she shook it awake, and followed it down to the sea.

On this beach, however, the baby seal lay all alone. It was still there at high tide, still there at twilight. A little white lump that trembled as it breathed. Through the night we thought of it crawling and crying, shivering in the wind of a coming storm. We thought of the eagles that would sink their talons into its flesh, that would perch atop it and tear out those eyes that were like pools of warm treacle. And when morning came, we were afraid to go down and look.

The wind had scattered the cardboard, the waves and the tide had washed away the little manger and smoothed out the scuff marks from the gravel. A few feet away, the baby seal lay on its side, suckling in its sleep. Everyone from the village agreed: it would die if we left it there any longer.

When we picked him up for the trip to town, for the start of his journey south to professional care in Vancouver, he curled his flipper around our fingers, and held on.

It was a fisherman who had found him. That was the thing that touched me.

Today the fishermen struggle just to survive. The government has cut the fleet by half; it has restricted the fishing and shortened the season so that a man has only weeks in which to earn a year's living. Then he finds that a seal has stripped his trolling gear of all but the heads of the salmon, that a seal has swum down his net taking a bite from each fish. It's no wonder that he gets out his gun. It's no wonder he'd like to slaughter the seals.

But it was a fisherman who saved this one little orphaned baby. That is the thing I'll remember.

Becoming a Sailor

"You be Kristin," he said, and stepped from the cockpit to the cabin top. The boat swayed, and he steadied himself on the boom. "Now remember; you're Kristin," he said.

"Okay." I told him to put on his lifejacket. He said, "I don't need it." He was being me.

He moved forward, past the mast to the foredeck, where the spinnaker pole scythed side to side, long as a farm gate. He showed me what to do, how to lead the halyard and guys, where to stand so the pole wouldn't sweep me over the side. He looked at home up there, as the boat beetled to windward, but then, he should; he had raced boats across the Pacific under an acre of sail. The perfect person, I'd thought, to test a new spinnaker and set it up so I could use it with Kristin.

But he didn't like my system. "You've got too many strings," he said. They were everywhere: uphaul, downhaul and outhaul; halyard and guys and sheets. He told me I wouldn't have to bother with sails when the wind got a hold of all those lines.

At the mouth of the harbour, he became Kristin and I became me. I gave him the tiller, and he sat there scowling at the mess in the cockpit. "Tell me what to do," he said. "I'm Kristin; I don't know anything."

We turned off the motor and hoisted the spinnaker. It opened with a puff, like a cloud, like a flower unfurling. Kristin would have been thrilled, but he only grunted. My system of strings was a nest of angry snakes, twisting themselves around rigging and pole. But we were sailing, going at a rush down the harbour. Soon we were too close to the land for *his* liking. He said people could

see him from there. So we jibed the boat. The guy became the sheet and the sheet became the guy; the whole thing became an awful tangle.

And he became me again; he heaved himself up. "I'll try to sort out this mess," he said with a sigh.

He stood in the tangle as the boat plunged along, pulling on lines that had no ends, and he reminded me of Captain Ahab snared to the back of Moby Dick. I said, "You look like a man caught in a spider web." It was the sort of thing Kristin might have said. But he didn't answer; he was being me.

We took down the sail and started again. It went better the second time; even better the third. Then we ran down the harbour with the spinnaker, bulbous and huge, pulling us on. It didn't matter who saw us. We were a postcard boat scudding along.

"Looks good," he said. "A few more times and you might start to get the hang of it."

And I smiled. He'd become himself again and I'd become a down-wind sailor.

The Incredible Shrinking Island

IT WAS BIG ENOUGH AT ONE TIME TO HOUSE A WHOLE VILLAGE, though just a small one. But now you can walk right around Garden Island in a minute or two. Year by year, yard by yard, it's shrinking, and vanishing quickly into the harbour.

Maybe five thousand years ago, people came and lived on Garden Island. They cleared the western beach of every stone bigger than a fist, piling them in long strips; berms to land canoes between. The island was nearly round then, with just a bight on that side, like a gibbous moon floating at the harbour mouth. A moon that was then already on the wane.

It was just a tiny spit of land the first time we poled the skiff across the rock-peppered shoals and landed on its shore. We walked once around, then sat on the beach and watched the fishing boats stream through Metlakatla Pass. We crossed the center of the island, through a thick tangle of gorse bushes, and found a marble gravestone sitting flat on the beach.

He was a young man, I like to think, or not terribly old. He was one of Prince Rupert's pioneers, buried here in the city's first choice for a cemetery; on an island that was once a village.

It was a mystery to us how someone could be buried right at the waterline like that. It didn't occur to us at first that six feet of island had washed away below the grave stone, that eighty years of winter storms had washed away his grave, leaving the marble stone flat on the new beach.

We've only returned once or twice. Each time we found the island smaller, the shoals of the drowning village more vast. Where we'd sat and watched the fishboats pass, the beach had washed away.

One summer evening, among the rubble at the water's edge, I picked up a stone that had a curious shape, rather like a fish. Someone, centuries before, had carved little eyes side-by-side on its top.

I gave the stone to a director of the national museum. It was one of only five or six he'd ever seen, a Shaman's tool, he told us, used in a ceremony to bring the salmon in from the sea. He described it for us, making it magical and real, how the Shaman tied these stones about his waist and swam out from the island and back again. And then he told us a legend, of how the salmon come from the heavens.

When a person dies, the legend says, his soul goes up to join the millions of other souls that glitter in the band of light we call the Milky Way. They move in a crowd across the sky, past the Andromeda Galaxy and Canopus, jostled along as other souls come up behind, right to the end of the Milky Way, where they tumble down and land in the waters of the Nass River. They land in the shape of fish, their souls transformed to salmon.

This was an ancient stone I'd found. But the soul of the Shaman who carved it may still be up there, near Orion maybe, looking down at his little moon-shaped island waning in the harbour.

Whaling Again

IN THE MIDDLE OF THE MONTH, not far from home, we had whales for dinner. There were two of them, each one nearly twice the size of the boat, big as boxcars; two of the largest animals on earth.

We were on a tiny island of trees and moss amid rocks like dinosaur teeth. Threads of smoke from our driftwood fire spun up between the trees, rising into a white sky streaked with grey and violet. Folded satin, Kristin called it. We perched like salamanders on the jagged rocks and baked a salmon on the fire.

To the west, at the head of the bay where we'd anchored for the night, the land rose in vast slopes and ridges to a ring of peaks two thousand feet above us. Outside, the sea churned to a southeast swell, stretching on to distant mountains.

The whales came at sunset, when a red glow spread across the clouds and turned the sea into a bed of coals. They surfaced where the water was as deep as the hills were high. They burst from it in blasts of spray, black shapes rising on the swells. The sound of their breathing echoed across the water—a booming, metallic sound, like hammers on iron plates.

Side by side they rose from the sea, backs arching, glistening in the red light. Their spouts were dark like rain clouds, and still the whales came rising from the water in black humps that turned, and bent, and sank again. Then a huge tail flicked up, streaming water. When it disappeared, the whales were gone.

"They're the same ones, aren't they?" Kristin asked.

"Yes," I said. "I think so."

We'd seen them two days earlier and ten miles away, coming toward us, close to the shore. They'd passed us inside the line of kelp, just a few feet from the beach. We'd watched them for a long time, until they were just two black specks rising and falling on the water.

The whales surfaced again off our little island. Again we heard the blast of air and the whoosh as indrawn breath. The animals came rising up, so close to each other they might have been touching underwater, like a couple holding hands. Each one weighed forty tons.

Kristin had her back to me, watching them. They came up twice more, one like the shadow of the other, breath booming back from the hills. "Japan's started whaling again," she said. "Did you hear that?"

"No," I said. I saw her silhouette against the pink of the clouds, and beyond her the whales rising again. Each knew exactly what the other was doing, and when it would do it.

"They've lifted the quotas or something," she said.

She looked back and I turned away. The salmon was sizzling on the fire, bits of fat burning with orange flames. It was funny to think that the giant whales were feeding on microscopic plants.

They came up side by side once more, breathed together, sank together. A huge tail rose up once more, curled, then vanished.

Kristin stood among the shards of rock, watching. They'd gone deep, down where the water would be black as ink, two thousand feet down.

She came back to the fire as I stirred up the coals and sat beside me on a flat rock, staring at the little fire. Together, we sighed.

Tracking the Ghosts

IN THE SUMMER, we find ourselves following ghosts, tracking them through time from bay to bay. They're the ghosts of square-rigged ships, and men in jerseys with their hair tarred in pigtails. And everywhere we go, they've been there two hundred years before.

Late one evening, as the sun set behind us, we rounded a point named after one of the ghosts, and in the darkness we anchored there, just north of Namu. We dropped the hook in a blast of phosphorescence, in a green ball that sank down and streamed away in the current. The chain ran out, clattering over the bow roller, and then the line, singing up through the hawse, beads of light flying as it snaked down into the water. And then, from the dark hills around us, the rattle of the chain rang back from the trees, the only sound anywhere around.

Two centuries before, Captain Vancouver and the men of the *Discovery*, half a world from home, would have heard the same sounds echoing from the same hills. For we'd anchored at Fougner Bay, right above those ancient ghosts.

We swung around in the current, the line creaking as it drew taut. It stretched down at an angle through the water, shining with a green glow as the water streamed around it to gurgle past the bow in lines of emerald light.

Later, when the stars came out, we could see the barbs of silhouetted trees around the bay, and a flicker of blue on the snow of distant mountain peaks. From the head of the bay, we could hear water trickling out of a little stream.

Near its mouth, just a spot in the night, a single light bobbed against the darkened shore. If you looked long enough, the trees became the masts and spars of a full-rigged ship, and the light came shining through the windows of the *Discovery's* cabin, where, two hundred years ago Vancouver was scratching a quill across the pages of his diary.

> *Near this stream, by the felling of a few trees, a very good situation was obtained. The seine was hauled with considerable success, so that we had a prospect of much convenience, and of acquiring some refreshment from the sea.*
>
> *These were advantages far beyond our expectations in this desolate region, where the rain had been almost incessantly pouring down in torrents ever since our arrival on it.*

In the morning we went our separate ways , the ghosts going inland with their huge sails sagging from the yards, Kristin and I fishing across the channel mouth—without considerable success—and wandering along our way.

When we anchored near dark we were ten miles apart. *Nid* swung all alone in a cove strewn with rocks. *Discovery* lay tied by a shore, and in its own lonely spot the sounds of hammering and spectral laughter must have rung through the hills. In the twilight, with no one there to see, the ghosts were stripping copper from the sides of their ship. They were repairing a leak at the bow, and they'd been given an extra ration of spirits to cheer themselves so far from home.

The Friendly Porpoise

WE CALLED HIM THE FRIENDLY PORPOISE. He was just a little guy, his belly more brown than white. He latched onto us thirty miles south of Oona River and stayed with us all morning.

He came from behind, as porpoises often do, suddenly appearing in a flash of black close under the surface. There was a shout of air as he snatched a breath, then rolled on his side and passed below the keel.

We always love that, to see the porpoises suddenly pop from the water with the suddenness of rabbits pulled from a hat. They often come in groups of four to six to play like children around the boat. They take turns crossing the bow, darting past in a stream of bubbles, surfacing under the bowsprit with a burst of spray. Each one comes a little closer, until you can lie on the foredeck, reaching down, and almost touch them as they pass.

But the friendly porpoise came alone. It seemed to us he didn't want to play, but just find companionship with other mammals.

We'd read the works of Dr. Lilly. We'd seen *Day of the Dolphin.* So we tried to establish communications with the friendly porpoise, to set up a dialogue, to build a rapport. If it was intelligent company he was seeking, he must have been sadly disappointed.

We blew whistles for him. We shouted and cheered. We dangled our hands in the water and thumped on the hull. But the friendly porpoise kept swimming up and down the length of the boat as we plowed along through Principe Channel.

Again and again he passed slowly from the stern, barely below the surface, then rolled on his side to slip past the cockpit. He turned one eye toward us, one huge eye, looking up as we looked down. He passed within inches of our outstretched arms, our fingers tickling the water.

The friendly porpoise at our side, we swung off into Petrel Channel. We opened a can of sardines as we headed north and threw scraps of the oily fish in the water whenever he came close alongside. He flashed by, spiraling slowly, without a sniff at the sardines. Bit by bit, we threw half the sardines in the water, but made no progress at all toward inter-species communication.

Halfway up McCauley Island, with a fair wind blowing us home, the friendly porpoise suddenly turned and shot off the way we had come. We were left with nothing but the story of a strange encounter. We felt as though we had met an ambassador from another world and almost, but not quite, learned the workings of that place.

Remembering Madeline

I'LL ALWAYS REMEMBER MADELINE. She was meek and quiet, like the women of the old television shows, an Edith Bunker to the Archie on the flying bridge. Her face was at the window as their boat came into the harbour, a pale shape turning behind the glass, like those crystals that people hang from strings to catch the light.

He looked like the sort of man who would introduce Madeline as his first mate, who would decorate his boat with little plaques saying "The Captain is Always Right." He came down from the bridge as they approached the anchor site and turned away from shore. He kicked the anchor free from its chock. He turned to shout orders at her, in big capital letters with lots of exclamation marks.

"PUT IT IN REVERSE!" he said, and the boat shuddered to a stop, slid backward as Madeline worked the controls.

He dropped the anchor and kicked at the chain as it rattled out. Fathoms and fathoms went clattering over the roller. Then he leaned on the bow railing as the boat backed down toward the shore, as Madeline glanced anxiously over her shoulder. When the boat was only a few yards from beaching, he looked up at Madeline and yelled:

"WHAT THE HELL ARE YOU DOING!" he said. "YOU'RE STILL IN REVERSE!!"

Madeline's voice didn't even carry over the water. She was staring at him with eyes like clamshells as her mouth worked silently.

"I DIDN'T THINK I'D HAVE TO TELL YOU TO PUT IT IN NEUTRAL," he said. "NOW WE HAVE TO SET THE ANCHOR AGAIN!" He swore at her again, then bent down and brought in the anchor, stopping when it broke the surface. "GO FORWARD ON THE PORT ENGINE!" he said.

Behind the glass, Madeline's face caught the light.

"THE PORT ENGINE!!" And he gestured wildly at the throttles, his finger poking at the air. "THAT ONE!!!"

There was a click of speakers then, and Madeline's voice came over a loud-hailer, quavering and high: "We've got no forward or reverse on the port engine."

"OH NO!!!!" He slammed his hand down on the cabin roof. He stormed down the deck. "MOVE OVER!!!!" he snarled, and flung himself into the wheelhouse.

Poor Madeline scuttled aside, her hands fluttering like birds. He grabbed the throttles in his fists and jammed them forward and back, and a moment later the boat was surging forward again, and he was back on the deck giving his pants a hitch where they sagged round his belly. There was nothing wrong with the engine; it seemed that Madeline, in her meekness, just hadn't pushed hard enough. Now she stood at the window again, her face grim and unmoving, as though etched in a frosted pane.

There were other boats in the harbour, and every one was hushed and terribly quiet. People stood and watched, heads shaking as they mourned for Madeline.

In the end he anchored out where there was room to swing, room to bellow and shout with no one there to hear. The engine switched off, and silence came to the bay.

For Madeline, the worst was over. Each day she would dread the anchoring that would come at the end. Or the docking; she would dread that even more. With the anchor down she would bustle about, fetching the captain's beer, seeing to the captain's dinner, collecting those things the captain had scattered in his fury. I thought, Madeline is exactly where she wants to be, just she and the captain in lonely exclusion. That would be Madeline's way, to herd this big boar of a man with little tweaks at his snout and his tail. No, there was nothing wrong with the engine. And Madeline had known it herself.

I remember her now when tensions start to build on our own little boat. I say her name over and over like an incantation when I stumble over Kristin's boots in the night or crack my head on the hatch that she left ajar.

"Madeline. Remember Madeline," I mutter to myself.

For tensions have a way of building on a small boat like gasoline fumes. They collect in the low spots, slowly thicken and build. It doesn't take much to set them off—a flicker of anger or a spark of annoyance is enough. Then words fly like bits of shrapnel, and in the end there's a fallout of strained and awful silence.

Kristin has her own ways of dispersing the fumes, ways that are better than mine, for it rarely bothers her when I snap at her over nothing at all or sit in long, brooding silences.

We have a pretty happy little ship, all in all, thanks to Kristin's patience. And my remembering Madeline.

A Saint in Humpback Bay

THERE WAS ONE OTHER BOAT IN HUMPBACK BAY when we stopped there for the night. A sloop, a bit bigger than *Nid,* it lay to a small float suspended between dolphins, a bit of old dock silvered by sun. It was cluttered with gear—it had come a long way—but there was no sign of anyone as we motored on past to drop the anchor in the mud and log chips of the bay.

I took a bottle of beer into the cockpit and nestled down with my back against the mainsheet. I sat and watched the shore slowly revolve as *Nid* turned with the current. The buildings of the old cannery, white-washed and tin-roofed, swung past the mast; the Lawyer Island light followed the Ada Islands, Chatham Sound went slowly by. We'd turned right around, back toward the cannery wharves, when the cry came across the water.

"Ship ahoy!"

No one had ever hailed me quite like that before and I must have reacted rather slowly, because I was "ship ahoyed" again before I could turn around. On the float beside the sailboat stood a small, elfish man, a gnome of a man in khaki shorts and socks to his knees. He was studying me through binoculars though we were only fifty yards apart.

"Could you give me some assistance?" he called in a plaintive sort of voice. I set my bottle down and paddled across in the inflatable dinghy.

The sailor was 74, ten days older than he'd been when he sailed through the narrow gap into Humpback Bay. He'd spent more than a week tied to that weathered old float, waiting for a wind that would take him across to the shipyard in Port Edward. He couldn't run his motor—it was rattling and shaking like a piledriver—and he'd spent the time peering down through the water at a tangle of cords bunched round the propeller shaft, poking at it with bits of stick.

"Do you think it's rope?" he asked. "Does it look like rope?"

It looked like kelp, but he hoped it was rope. There were only a few coils wrapped around the shaft, enough rope to jam the little engine, but not enough kelp to make any difference at all. If the coils turned out to be rope, he could strip them off and be on his way. If they turned out be kelp, his problem was inside the engine.

"Do you have something," he asked, "that would reach it?"

I took the small boathook from the dinghy and fished around in the water. It thunked against the shaft; its hook snared in the tangles. The sailor pulled on a rubber face mask and dunked his head under the water.

When he surfaced again, I gave him the news. "It's kelp."

He blinked at me through the face mask. "Are you sure?"

"Sure," I said. Chunks of leaf and slimy tubes of stalk bubbled like chowder on the surface.

He looked sadly at the broken kelp and resigned himself, I suppose, to an expensive stop at a shipyard. Then he smiled, and shrugged, and invited me aboard for a glass of wine.

I love seeing the inside of people's boats. They're the measure of the owner. In his house, a man keeps a vast collection of things, but in his boat he picks and chooses, selecting only the things that define him.

And this one was Spartan: simple and plain. The woodwork—all square-cornered, either vertical or flat with no bends and no scrollwork—filled the boat from the sides nearly right to the center. He had a narrow strip of floor just wide enough for a pair of feet. He slept in a narrow bunk, below a Plexiglas dome that let him lift his head for a look around.

The boat was only twenty-nine feet long, but had been his home for nine years, since the death of his wife. Before the day he bought it, he'd never once gone sailing.

He kept no pictures, no baubles, no seashells or feathers. A small bookshelf contained all the volumes of *The Lives of the Saints* and little else. He read them lying down or standing up; there were no seats on the boat. He even ate his meals standing up, which wasn't much of a hardship since the only food he ever carried was peanut butter and glucose, and fruit-flavored Tang. He showed me his supplies, the three little jars.

I said, "That's your whole galley?"

"Yes," he said. "It's all I need."

He tapped two glasses of red wine from a cardboard box and we drank a toast to our respective voyages. He was heading south from Alaska, travelling alone as he always had, as he always would. We drank the wine, and talked about the saints, and he kept opening the books, one after the other, his eyes aglow as he fondled the pages. He was like a man showing off family albums.

In the morning, we motored past him and out through the gap. He didn't want a tow; he was happy to wait as long as it took for the wind to turn fair. He wanted a westerly, and he would sit there until it came, until he could raise his sails and climb on the wind, and ride it out of Humpback Bay.

That was years ago. But I still think of him when I see a boat like his, and I picture him in some quiet cove reading from a big, yellowed book about Saint Erasmus or Saint Francis, standing and reading, as he spoons peanut butter from the jar.

He was so quiet, so very alone. So content in a boat without comfort. His whole life was spent marvelling at the ways of the world, travelling with the wind and the weather as though he was part of it all, a tiny spring in the clockwork of the universe.

I can't help thinking that maybe I did meet a saint that evening in Humpback Bay. Another Saint Brendan, searching for a mysterious land far from human ken, and finding paradise at the end—a lonely paradise, but paradise none the less. And he is there now—he will always be there—sailing from island to island, from the fog to the sky, close-hauled through the clouds on a reach through the stars.

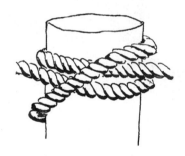

Compliments of the Alaskans

KRISTIN WAS PICKING BERRIES ALONG A WINDING TRAIL when she met the Alaskans, a man and his wife returning to their boat after an afternoon on the beach. They stopped to talk for a moment as they squeezed past her in a thicket of huckleberries.

"Is that your friend on the beach?" the woman asked. "With the little dog?"

"Yes," said Kristin.

The woman nodded. "Well," she said, "you sure have a cute dog."

Kristin laughed when she told me that, standing in the sand with a bucket of red berries in one hand, a bucket of blue berries in the other. She said, "He has a big beard, like a sourdough miner. You'll probably meet them later."

In the evening, we passed the Alaskans on the trail. They had a black Labrador that trotted ahead of them with a bit of wood in its mouth, sleek like an otter and five times the size of our little Skipper. And they stopped, again, to admire our dog and say how pretty she was.

"She's very friendly," he said, bending down to pet her.

The next day, we passed once more on the trail, and the Alaskans complimented us on the mounds of berries we'd picked that morning. Late that afternoon, they rowed past the boat in a brand new Zodiac and stopped to wave. We were loading our old dinghy for dinner on the beach. Kristin stood in the half-deflated boat, stowing things away as I passed them down to her.

The man rested on his oars, his beard lying across his knees. For a moment, I thought he was admiring the Dutch oven as I handed it to Kristin. But he called out across the water, "I like your cutter."

"Eh?" Kristin said, and frowned. She pointed at the dinghy, patched like a pair of hobo pants, sagging limply around her ankles. "THIS?"

"No. Your cutter," he said. "She's a cutie."

"Thank you," I said.

Kristin packed away the Dutch oven and climbed out of the dinghy. "I didn't know this was a cutter," she said.

"Sure," I told her. "Just like theirs." I watched the Alaskans row off toward their boat. Anchored behind us, it sparkled in the sun like a huge emerald. Its cutter rig was the only thing it had in common with our Nid. I'd sat in the starlight the night before, just staring at it.

"They're very nice," Kristin said. "The Alaskans."

Yes," I said. They'd complimented us on almost everything we owned, though they could match each item with something bigger, something shinier and newer. I'd met few people like that, genuinely pleasant people who owned things I can only dream of having. Generally, I hate people like that.

"He's very complimentary, isn't he?" Kristin said.

"Yes, he is." I got out the ancient bellows and puffed up the dinghy enough to get us to the beach and back.

"Maybe," she said, "we should row over and admire something of theirs."

"I don't think so," I said.

The next day, the Alaskans left the anchorage. They circled our boat on the way out, their big diesel purring quietly as a cat. When they waved, I waved back.

"That's a beautiful boat," I said.

The man was clinging to the backstay, his beard blowing back, rippling against his cheeks. "Why, thank you," he said. And the way he smiled, you'd think no one had ever told him that before.

Gale Warning

THE ISLANDS ARE SMALL AND BARREN, just a smudge on the chart, and a smear of blue on the horizon. For four days we sat and stared at them—or at the line of dark clouds that hovered above them—as southeast winds blew up the gap between us and the Goose Islands.

In our imaginations, they became a wonderful land where people seldom went, where the beaches were sand and stretched forever, littered with glass balls that had drifted all the way from Japan. And on the fifth day, when the weather broke, we slipped across to the Goose Islands and dropped the anchor in water so clear that I could watch it set in the sand four fathoms down.

Then we looked around us, at the big motor yacht anchored nearby, at the tents strung along the beach. To our left, a lone kayaker was hacking up bits of driftwood for his campfire. And to the right, a skiff-load of men stepped ashore with deer rifles.

By nightfall, there were four other boats in the anchorage, and the radio was calling for southeast gales.

"You don't want to be out there if it blows southeast," the man in the cabin cruiser had told us. He'd found us three days before, as we waited for the weather. He was the only person we'd seen in more than a week.

"There's no protection there," he'd said. "And you can't run back because the tide flows out through these inlets and sets up incredible waves. It's dangerous. Very dangerous."

In the morning, the wind backed to the south. The kayaker had already left, and the tents had vanished from the beach. High, shredded clouds filled the sky, and where the sun shone through, dimly, there was a big ring around it, like a halo.

"What does that mean?" Kristin asked.

"Wind," I said.

One by one, the powerboats were leaving. We heard them go, in a rattle of chain and a rumble of engines, saw them bounding over the waves like frightened deer at the sound of a gunshot.

"At least we have the place to ourselves now," said Kristin. We moved the boat and anchored again close to the cliff of a small island on the edge of the anchorage. We put out a stern anchor, and a line to shore.

"Winds rising this afternoon," the radio said, "to southeast two-five to gales three-five."

With the boat pinned in place like a bug on a mounting board, we could look out the hatch and over the stern to the nearest land almost ten miles away. The island would break the wind, but not the swells that were forecast to build to seven feet or more during the night.

"You don't want to be out there if it blows southeast," the man had told us. "And you can't run back."

We walked along the beach, and watched the clouds coming in low bands toward us. They snagged long wisps in the trees, stretched grey fingers toward the water.

In the afternoon, the sea was a cold, dull blue, and masses of kelp came drifting in on swells that churned and burst among the rocks. Fifty miles to the south, it was already blowing forty knots.

The rain started then, and we thought of leaving before the gale arrived, of hoisting the sails and running north like a big seabird spreading its wings and heading inland on the wind.

But we stayed instead, tied all the mooring lines and bits of rope together and stretched them to a tree on shore, lowered lead balls on the anchor chain, and watched the sky.

"You can't run back . . . "

Through the afternoon and into the evening, the clouds gathered overhead. They were thick and dark, the edges feathered as they drove along on the wind.

Then, just before sunset, the sky to the west flashed with golden light and rays, like searchlight beams, flickered across the sky making trapezoid shapes on the bottom of the clouds and flickering on the water. We saw the sun, for just a moment, and then the redness came. It was the color of roses and burgundy wine, deep and rich. And we knew we were safe then, through the night.

In the morning, the gale warning was cancelled. We rowed the dinghy to shore and hauled it high up on a beach that went on forever, where the only footprints were our own, and people seldom came.

Storing Our Little Souvenirs

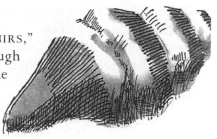

"**T**HAT'S THE PROBLEM WITH SOUVENIRS," said Kristin. "There's never enough places to put them." She was watching me pack away the latest treasures found on the beach, the little souvenirs that would remind us of the south.

"It'll fit," I said.

"Oh, I'm sure it will," she said, and laughed. And I wrenched on the legs of the armchair, and it jammed halfway into the quarter berth.

It had been lying on its back in the sand, the blue plastic scored by rocks and barnacles. A strand of seaweed had been wrapped round and round the legs.

"Well, I can't leave this behind," I'd said and carried it on my back through a mile of bush, looking like the mad trapper, I suppose, with this huge chair snagging on every branch and twig. But I'd got it back, and I'd stood it up in the cockpit and sat there, wondering where I'd put it.

I yanked it out from the quarter berth and peered inside. It seemed most of our little souvenirs had ended up in there and now they were in a hopeless jumble.

"It's this canning kettle of yours," I said, thumping the thing with my fist. It was about the size of a drum—a kettle drum, maybe—and Kristin had wrapped it carefully in a jacket so the enamel wouldn't chip. "I'll use your jacket, all right?" she'd said. "After all, it was your mother who gave us the kettle."

It was true. Mom had hauled it up Vancouver Island in the trunk of the car. "Of course there'll be room for it," I'd told her. "I'll just put it in the quarter berth."

The problem was, it was getting blocked by the big foam slab, the largest of our little souvenirs. I gave it a poke, trying to cram it down a little farther.

The big foam slab was wrapped in plastic and wedged right under the cockpit. "We might be glad we've got that," Kristin had said as she stuffed it back there. "We don't have any other spare foamies." And I'd thought at the time that it was just as well.

So I shoved the canning kettle back in place and squeezed the armchair into the bow, onto the berth that stretches the width of the boat. "There," I said.

Kristin peered over the bulkhead, her hands clutched on the top edge. She looked like a Kilroy figure. "That better not be on my side," she said.

"You won't even know it's here," I said, and twisted the arms until the chair popped down under the bookshelf. There was lots of room left for the last of our little souvenirs—an ice chest I'd found on the beach.

It had been sitting on the sand, not far from the armchair, surrounded by fading footprints half-swept by wind and pock-marked by rain. I'd knelt down beside it, like a boy with a treasure chest, and pried open the lid. Not only had there been two cans of beer inside, but they were still cold. I'd picked up the cooler in one hand, the armchair in the other, and set off up the beach.

"You look like a Yuppie," Kristin had said. "No. You look worse than a Yuppie."

So I shoved the ice chest behind the armchair, and stuffed the canning kettle in with the big foam slab, and all our little souvenirs were safely tucked in place.

"You're finding all the good stuff," Kristin said. And from that moment, it seemed, she always had the binoculars in her hands, scanning the shoreline in every direction. She looked like a U-boat captain on patrol.

"Look," she said, a few days later. There was something white on the beach, up amongst the rocks. Kristin polished the lenses and fiddled with the focusing knob. "It's a bathtub! There's a great big bathtub on the beach."

"Really?" I said. And I reached down, and jammed the throttle open.

Graveside Visitors

ON THE CHART IT WAS CALLED GREEN NECK. It was a narrow strip of land with an anchorage on each side and a jungle of thimble berry and black currant bushes in the middle.

There was a little beach of shells and gravel, and an old log house with gingerbread trim around the door. Crab-apples grew beside the house, and huge cherry trees towered in a grove beside the beach.

The man who built the house had planted a garden around it—the fruit trees and the currant bushes. And when he'd died, they'd buried him there in his grove of cherry trees and marked the spot with a simple wooden cross.

It was a place we returned to year after year, and we smiled to see it again as we anchored in the bay on a summer afternoon.

The man's house was still there, his crab-apple trees and currant bushes. But someone had stolen the cross that marked his grave. And someone had done some digging around in his grove of cherry trees.

At high tide, we built a fire on the beach. We sat back in the shells and watched a group of kayakers come in around the point, their paddles seesawing and dipping at the water. From a distance, they looked like big beetles, like water-boatmen.

"Company's coming," I said, sorry that we had to share the spot with someone else.

"That's all right," said Kristin. "There's lots of room." And she put another stick on the fire.

But the kayakers came straight toward us, insects drawn by the fire, and landed on the beach only a foot away. There were four adults and a child, and they started unloading tents and camping gear, piling it all beside us.

One of them asked if we were staying for the night. We said no, only for dinner, and he nodded. "Don't let us rush you," he added politely.

Another walked up behind the fire and trampled in the grass. "This is a good spot for the tents," she said, and cast down a bundle of aluminum poles.

Kristin leaned closed toward me. "This is a bit much," she said. "There's a whole empty coast here."

"This is a nice spot," the first kayaker said. "It's a good beach."

"Yes," said Kristin. "It goes on for a long way, on both sides."

The kayaker looked around, and nodded. "Yes, it does," he said.

And we all sat there for a while, Kristin and I around our fire, the kayakers a few feet away, waiting for us to leave. The smoke eddied around them, in wisps at first, and then in clouds when I threw wet bark on top to make the coals.

Two of the kayakers wandered up the beach and back. They held a conference then, and started collecting their tents and gear.

"We've found another spot," one of them said. "It'll give us all a bit more room." The others trundled by with pans and sleeping bags. "Yes," he said. "There's a nice place just over there. See?" He pointed. "In that grove of cherry trees."

We looked at each other, Kristin and I.

"There's someone buried there," I said, and they all stopped, bundles in their hands, like a line of shoppers in a sporting goods store.

"Where all that digging is?" he asked.

"No, no," Kristin said. "The grave is further back. It won't be in your way. Really."

But I wasn't surprised when they decided not to camp in the grove of cherry trees after all. They cooked their dinner on a Coleman stove a few yards from us, off in the other direction.

After dinner, we did sit down with the kayakers. They were just setting out along the same route we'd used earlier in the summer, and we talked about different places along the way.

I gave them a little map, to make amends, and marked interesting places on it for them. Kristin offered them an extra tarp, for the weather didn't look good at all. And after a while, Skipper the dog even stopped growling at their little girl.

We talked until the sunset. And then they all stood along the shore waving to us as we paddled off in the dinghy.

"Come and have breakfast with us," one of them said. "You're the first yachters we've enjoyed."

That made me feel really bad. "They must have met some pretty awful people," I said.

Lost at Sea

WE FOUND A SPIDER ON THE BOAT, a small one with grand ideas. He lounged in a hammock hung from the windvane, and he raised a hand or two in greeting, inviting us to step aboard.

I went to the stern and stood at the rail, and he hauled himself up from his hammock. He took a gossamer halyard from its pinrail then swung himself, like Errol Flynn, across the gap from vane to pulpit. And he paced there, back and forth, all alone on his quarter deck.

There was no miserly landlubber's web for him; his was a palace that filled the stern, a triple-decker with railings and lifelines. He had a drawing room on the transom, a sundeck on the anchor, a parlor in the pulpit. He even had a single silvery strand flying from the masthead like a commodore's pennant.

I called him Conrad.

He seemed happy to have people aboard, a crew to tend the ship as he went about his affairs. He had the boarding nets slung out and kept himself busy repelling flies from the stern, his arms whirling like saber blades.

We brought aboard our things and readied the boat, and Conrad bustled back and forth, lashing down his gear. We motored round for fuel and water, and there was Conrad, watching from the backstay.

In four days we were ready to leave. Kristin found me kneeling on the deck, corralling Conrad in my hands.

"What are you doing?" she asked.

It seemed obvious to me. "Time for the spider to go ashore."

But Kristin would have none of that. "Leave him," she said. "He's a lucky spider."

And so we went to sea on a Saturday, a crew of two and Conrad.

We sailed up Puget Sound and across the Strait, and anchored in the San Juans. "A long day," said Kristin, lying back in the cockpit. But poor Conrad went dashing off to repair the damage done by mooring lines and windvane. He spent the night huddled under the rubrail, but was up again at first light, shaking the dew from his hammock and seining for flies on the morning set.

As we headed north in rising winds, plunging through the tide rips of Haro Strait, Conrad went crawling out on the stern roller to add extra lines. He clung to his web in a fearless way, with seven hands for the boat and one for himself. And when we went through customs at Sidney, he didn't bother going ashore. He was a sea-going spider, born on the boat.

In the Gulf of Georgia, the weather thickened. Whitecaps charged alongside us like stampeding horses. The waves grew higher and steeper, and we ran before a gale hour after hour, plunging down the waves, rising on their backs, reeling in the gusts. Water slammed against the transom, flinging spindrift in the air. It rumbled over the bow and coursed down the decks. The wind tore through Conrad's cabin and ripped his hammock into shreds. There was no sign of the spider. I imagined he'd lashed himself down in the lee of the rubrail and was riding there laughing, squinting at the wind.

We anchored behind Rebecca Spit, in a harbour white with spray. Halyards rattled on the mast, and the rigging sang like sirens in the wind.

And Conrad was gone.

I rowed around the boat, but he wasn't there. He wasn't tucked under the rail; he hadn't sheltered in the tubes of the windvane support.

"He jumped ship," I said.

"That's a euphemistic way to put it," said Kristin.

It was. Only today, when I saw the ragged remains of his hammock splattered on the transom and speckled with the flies he loved, could I finally face the truth.

Conrad the spider was lost at sea.

Dreaming of the Charlottes

IN PORT HARDY, ON A HOT SUMMER DAY, we found a young couple sleeping at the head of the fishermen's wharf. The woman lay against the man, and they both lay atop their backpacks, as though the sun had melted them into a blob on the planks. On a piece of cardboard propped beside them, they'd written a note begging a ride by boat to the Charlottes.

We imagined they'd come from Victoria, hitchhiking north to the end of the road, to the top of the island, determined to get to this place beyond the horizon. We imagined they were dreaming of the islands now as they slept in the sun, seeing blue peaks and green forests, old totems and beaches without footprints, everything half hidden in a swirl of cool mist.

I said, "I wish we could take them."

"But we're not going to the Charlottes," said Kristin.

"That's what I mean," I told her.

For seven years we've talked of going to the Queen Charlotte Islands. Each April or May the charts spread open like spring flowers, and in our minds we sail into the inlets and fjords of the Misty Isles.

Each summer we get to the edge of Hecate Strait and stare west at the cloud banks that form over a land we can't see, a night and a day beyond the horizon. The sixty-mile crossing would take us nearly twenty-four hours in our gaff-rigged old whaleboat. It's a daunting idea. It's a perilous crossing.

The Strait was named for a goddess of the night and the lower world, a goddess prayed to by witches. Hecate commanded all the powers of nature: the winds and the tides and the storms.

We've met two sailboats that were dismasted in Hecate Strait. One, a big cruiser on a round-the-world voyage from Germany, rolled right over in the shallows at the north end, and snapped her mast on the bottom. The other, a trimaran, drifted upside down for fourteen days in huge seas at the southern end. We've seen the fishboats come home in convoy over the Strait; we've known men who drowned out there.

And we've read *The Sea is for Sailing*, by Peter Pye, an English doctor who sailed a box of a boat sixty years old. Forty years ago he was among the first of the yachtsmen to visit the Charlottes merely for pleasure, the first in a hundred years to arrive from England. He recorded his landfall like this:

> *Dark pines clung to almost impossible slopes which rose into mist and cloud. Cold, bleak and wet. And yet to me, as we sailed into this deep fiord, it was more exciting than anything I had seen before. It was the remoteness, the savagery of the place, a thing I cannot do justice to in words.*

And this is how he left:

> *Never have I seen weather change in so short a time or in so sinister a manner.*

In two hours he went from full sail to four reefs.

> *The Hecate Strait was living up to its reputation: the wind howling out of the sou'east, the smoking sea, steep and ugly as if it was scooping the very mud off the bottom, the ship blinded by the fury of the elements. Sail had to come off. With infinite care, for our lives depended upon it, we got the mainsail down, lashing gaff and boom to gallows. Turning, we ran under bare poles towards the Dixon Entrance.*

But she ran too fast, and he payed out the warps—sixty fathoms of heavy rope.

> *And I knew that if I could keep the vessel off the rocks that she would still be afloat in the morning.*

We've been to the Charlottes, on the ferry. We've drunk faithfully from St. Mary's Spring, below the figure of the wooden lady. And according to legend, that means we'll return. But when we do, it will be in our own boat. We'll anchor off village sites where the totems still stand, and walk in quicksands of moss. We'll fill our water tank from mountain streams, and sail in and out of the mists.

And I think when we get there we'll find the people we met at Port Hardy.

Squid Jiggin'

IT WAS A CLEAR NIGHT, WITH A SKY FULL OF STARS and the water so clear they seemed to float there too—all around us, above and below—as though we'd found an anchorage in the heavens, a million miles from home. Across the narrow island, surf broke on a sandy beach, and somewhere in the darkness of the trees, an animal cried.

Kristin was leaning over the side of the boat, dipping her toothbrush in the water. Wherever she touched the surface, a bloom of light appeared, a burst of green. It came from microscopic animals that had gathered by the million, creatures that—disturbed—reacted with pulses of light. Kristin dabbled and laughed, delighted for the thousandth time by this display of phosphorescence.

But suddenly she drew back her hand. "Oh!" she said. "Look at this."

There were streaks in the reflected sky, tiny comets dashing between the stars. Kristin reached down again and stirred the water, and the rays of light flashed in all directions.

"What's doing that?" she said.

"Probably little fish." We'd seen them before, streaming emerald wakes through masses of the phosphorescent plankton.

"It doesn't look like fish." She peered at the water. "Do you think they'd show up better in the flashlight?"

"I doubt it," I said, not wanting to move.

"Try it anyway," she said, and waited there, bent over the gunwale, while I brought up the light and shone it at the water. The beam went down a long way, through clouds of swirling dust, and we could see strange animals, torpedo-like, flitting across the light.

Kristin barely whispered. "What are they?"

"Squid," I said.

There were dozens of them, all around the boat, swimming quickly just below the surface. The light attracted them, and repelled them at the same time, so that I could move the beam back and forth and pin them there, like actors in flood lights, and make them dance.

We talked, as we watched the double-ended squid, of how we might catch some and cook them for breakfast. Kristin told me how she'd done that as a child, eating squid her father would catch on summer camping trips.

"You jig for them," she said. "You use a thing with dozens of barbs, and you jerk it up until you snag them. Then you fry them in butter. And, oh, they're delicious."

I watched them dance in the light. "How do you kill them?"

"Hmmm," she said. "I don't know." She looked down, and her eyes followed the flashlight beam. "We can't very well bonk them over the head, because we don't know where the head is. I guess you just leave them in a bucket of water."

She set to work the next morning, folding squid jigs out of a torn-open pop can. All morning she folded and cut and twisted the shiny metal. Sometime around noon, she held up a weird sculpture tapering to slender tentacles.

"There." She turned it until it caught the sun. "Does that look like a squid?"

"No," I said.

She held it at arm's length. She squinted at it. "Maybe it does," she said, "if you're another squid."

She put it aside and pulled out the boating books to leaf through worn pages of recipes. And as she read, Skipper the dog carried off the jig and chewed it into a little ball of crumpled aluminum.

"Oh well," said Kristin. "I guess we can just dip them up with the net." She set it in the cockpit, ready for instant use, and waited for dark.

"You pin them in the light," she said, "and I'll dip them."

At sunset she filled a bucket with water to drop the squid in, and crouched at the rail, staring down, with the flashlight in her hand. An hour later she was still there, reaching for the net every time the water rippled close alongside.

"Oh, where are you, squid?" she said, in a plaintive voice.

Close to midnight, Kristin gave up the hunt. She lashed the oddly twisted net back in place and went sadly to bed. "I don't understand it," she said. "I just don't understand it."

As a child she'd loved her camping trips, her dinners of squid cooked over a smoky fire. Those were the times she talked about more than any other. And that night, I think, she'd hoped to be a child again, for an hour at least.

In the end she got that chance. A year later, almost to the day, we were anchored in that same place when the squid came bubbling around the boat. They came at dawn instead of at night, and they looked smaller in the daytime, like minnows wrapped in cellophane robes, like little fish turned to angels. We had her father's jigs hanging on hooks then, bright-colored ornaments of chartreuse and crimson bristling with silver barbs, the same ones she'd used in those long-ago summers. She fitted them on a line and went squid-jigging again.

We pulled up a dozen, and they wriggled and squirmed as they came from the sea. They shot squirts of black ink over the decks and our clothes, over our hands and our arms and our faces. They swam in a bucket of grey, and we put a lid on top and weighted it down; Kristin had also remembered how you kill them. Inside, they struggled and splashed. Their little bodies thumped at the lid.

"Now we go away and wait for a while," she said. "I remember now I didn't like this part very much."

But that evening we sat on the beach, at the edge of the surf. We built a fire of smoky old wood, and sat in the sand eating angel wings, laughing like children.

"We anchored in the late afternoon off a beach of sand and gravel at the bottom of an island."

Summer Reading

W E WERE SAILING ALONG NICELY, the sheets taut and water gurgling past the hull, when I asked Kristin to steer for a while. She slid over and grasped the tiller in her hand, then reached for the chart. "Just keep going straight," I said, stepping down into the cabin.

"Very well," she said in a brisk, seaman-like way that made me stop and look back at her. She glanced up. "Carry on," she said. And I knew then that she'd been reading sea stories again.

It happens every summer at some point, when she's exhausted all the books on her side of the little shelf in the bow. She fills the space with *Sea Microbes* and *Between Pacific Tides*, weighty tomes that make the boat tilt several degrees to that side. Kristin's biological degree, I call it, and counteract the weight with *The Sea Wolf* and *Devastation Island* and big, hefty books on stars and navigation.

Between them, in the middle of the shelf, go the second-hand paperbacks we collect during the year to salt away as provisions for our summer voyages. Stephen King is there, and Benjamin Franklin. Kristin read snatches of the statesman's memoirs every morning, like scripture readings, quoting them at odd times.

"Early to rise," she'd warble when the sun came in through the skylight and I'd have to climb out of bed and pump up the kerosene stove for the first pot of coffee.

When things were going wrong, and everything was breaking at once, she'd sigh and say: "Oh, I wish Ben was here. I'm sure he'd have something to say about all this."

When the brittle pages of Franklin's memoirs dropped out of its binding, and his *bons mots* lay scattered around the boat, Kristin went on through the next books on the shelf. She read *The Dionne Years* and, day by day, kept me informed of the growth of the famous quintuplets, until I felt like an old family friend.

Then, in desperation, she reached the Hornblower books at my end of the shelf, and we started talking to each other like 19th-century sailing masters: we didn't just start the engine, we "bent on the iron jib." We drank rum by the tot, and "belayed" the radio when there was nothing we wanted to hear. We told each other to "look smartly now" and to "keep your deadlights open" in the fog.

We replenished our book supply at Shearwater, before heading west through Gunboat Passage. I set the engine revolutions for three knots, rigged the boat for silent running, and carried on with *The Hunt for Red October* as I "conned" us slowly forward.

Kristin was reading *Gone With the Wind*. She started posturing in the companionway and sweeping down the steps like a hoop-skirted Scarlett. I gave her orders, but she wouldn't obey. All she would do was sit in the shade of the sails, fanning herself.

"I wish you'd go back to the sea stories," I told her.

"Frankly, my dear," she said. "I don't give a damn."

Son of Conrad

DO YOU REMEMBER CONRAD THE SPIDER
—lost at sea, torn from his web on the stern of
Connection, in a gale off Cape Mudge? A sad story.

He was so suddenly gone. Just that morning he'd
been a fellow rover, working with quiet pleasure at his fancy knots and splices.
Without him, the boat seemed diminished.

Poor Conrad. Oh, I suppose he might have made it to shore. He might
have spun himself a life raft and drifted for days—or weeks—until he washed
up on a lonely beach, to live a hermit's life on Quadra Island. But I doubt it. A
person can't survive for very long in those waters and, though I haven't seen
any studies done, I suspect it's worse for a spider.

So I tore away his webs when we got to Rupert. I tore them down and
threw them away, and they drifted off on the water like a silvery shroud.

And in the morning they were whole again.

It didn't seem possible. I took a stick, and swept it back and forth across the
transom, and the strands of web grew thick around it like cotton candy. I tore
down the hammock and the stern gallery; I shredded the little spider cuddy
from the base of the wind vane.

But in the morning the web was back.

It was a perfect web, a Conrad web, a wonderful macramé strung with
beads of icy dew. It filled with the breeze and emptied again, emptied and
filled, as I stood there staring. Right in the middle, where every line came
together, crouched a spider ghostly grey.

It wasn't Conrad, not the Conrad we'd known before. That one had been
a big strapping fellow, while this one was small and pale as a specter. But he'd
built his web in the very same spot, filling with silky lines the space abaft the
pulpit. I peered down at him, and he stared back with his little round spider
eyes. Then he lowered a line and scrambled down it, and swung aboard over
the stern.

And I knew then. This was the son of Conrad.

Apart from his size, he's every bit his father. He weaves his web with the
carrick bend and turtle knot, with zigzag running hitches. He preys with
piratical glee on blackflies and midges, bundling up their bodies every day at
dawn.

So I've left him there, in a stern cabin that grows bigger and grander week by week. He's even built a private gangway down to the dock, lashed in place with guys and mooring lines. Just like his dad: eight hands, and every one a marline spike.

Like any ship, we've found a routine. The spider takes the night watch, so I seldom see him. But in the evening I can lie in the berth below the cockpit and hear the little ticka-tick of his tiny legs going busily back and forth above me.

And as I sand and paint and varnish, I've come to believe that every boat should have a spider. Yesterday I painted the deck and left it to dry overnight. In the morning it was as hard and smooth as a frozen pond, and there wasn't a single fly speckled on the paint, not so much as a wing etched upon the grey.

He'd got them all, this son of Conrad.

The Boat That Died of Fear

SHE WAS A TINY BOAT, ALMOST A TOY REALLY, with a little cabin no bigger than a steamer trunk tipped on its end. Painted grey a long time ago, she was weathered now like an old sidewalk.

She'd worked the river for most of her life, and already she'd outlived the men who built her. Now she lay at the dock, rust weeping from every nail. People paused as they walked by and reached out to touch her, as they might stop for a moment to pet an old dog.

In a few years she'd be laid ashore, to rest on a grassy bank beside the water. I think she was waiting for that day, looking forward to it.

I liked to see her when I crossed from the far shore. She was always in the same spot, nestled in a corner of the wharf, an old, old lady watching and waiting.

Then I came to town one morning and saw her hatch covers moved aside, and men crouched over the engine that had sat silent for so long, its exhaust pipe capped by an old tomato can. In the evening, her usual spot was empty and I found her tied to a different dock, with a big man folded inside the little cabin. He looked up as I went by, and said hello.

"I'm going to New Zealand," he told me.

I said oh, yes, and he nodded and said he was going to put some drums of fuel on the deck so she could make the trip. He told me how he planned to take the little boat far off shore and maybe, he said, he'd flag down a freighter heading south. He said he'd leave her then, to fend for herself on the Pacific swells, and the words struck a chill in me.

"I think I'll put a mast on her, and some sails," he said. The hatch was open, and the small decks were strewn with bits of machinery covered in grease and rust. There were scraps of wood scattered around, and a tin can bristling with twisted nails.

"The hull's not bad," he said. "A bit of rot." And I saw he'd done some work already, tacking pieces of plywood over the planks like great, thick Band-Aids.

In a few days, he got the motor running, and it clattered and whirred in clouds of white smoke. The little boat jumped at the noise, shaking and twitching whenever it ran. She started leaking, too, plumes of oily brown water weeping from her bilges. She didn't want to go, it was plain to see.

But her owner took her for test runs in the harbour, training trips for the bluewater cruise. I'd see him, sometimes puttering away from the dock, but usually drifting back in with the engine dead again, and extra bumpers slung over the side.

He called it sailing. "I've already done more sailing than driving," he said.

I imagined he lay at night, crammed into the narrow hull, dreaming of New Zealand. I imagined he could picture the island's green mountains, and hear the pounding of the surf on its beaches.

But the little boat refused to go. She'd spent all her life on the river, in sheltered waters in the lee of land. That night, suddenly, she gave up the ghost, opened her seams and let the ocean in.

The man put her ashore on a shallow bank slick with grass and she rests there still. A little boat that died, not from age, but from fear.

Cross Porpoises

WE GLANCED UP WHEN THE OLD CHRIS CRAFT CAME gliding into the cove, faces in the windows like a line of store mannequins. We watched, scowling, as the only people for fifty miles around anchored just fifty feet away.

For days we'd waited there among unnamed islands, in the echo of booming surf, in a mist of salt spray that drifted across the thin band of trees. We'd shared the bay with porpoises and ravens, eagles and otters, and odd, mustached seabirds.

The birds vanished as the boat came in, engines throbbing, water gurgling and steaming at the exhaust outlets. I wondered how it was that our visitors had found their way here, like mosquitoes to a screened-in porch.

We shook our heads and frowned as they backed down toward the shore, blocking off the little creek where we dipped our water every day waiting for the weather to change.

Then the kids came out on deck, shrieking and shouting in excitement as they winched a Boston Whaler over the rail and dropped it in the water. We watched, sadly, as the boys climbed in and pulled the cover off a huge outboard. They had it running in a moment, the sound ringing through the bay where porpoises had played. Soon, they were fighting over who would get to steer, jostling each other at the steering wheel as the boat snaked and slewed across the water toward us.

"Great," I snarled

"Young hellions," said Kristin with a scowl.

The boat banked in a long curve, kicking up sheets of spray. It circled past the otter den, and roared back to the Chris Craft, where a man with binoculars waved to the boys from the foredeck. He pointed out to the channel. Standing in the boat as it rocked alongside, the kids looked out along his arm.

The porpoises were there, rising and falling in a tight circle, their backs glistening as they broke through the water with little spumes of breath. And with a whoop and a shrill cry, the boys raced off toward them.

"So much for the porpoises," I said.

The Boston Whaler shot out of the bay, skimming under a leaning tree where kingfishers had chattered in the evenings. The boat passed right over the porpoises and vanished behind the point.

We heard it roaring in circles, the boys' shouts rising over the scream of the engine. We couldn't see the porpoises any more at all.

"Poor things," said Kristin, while I glared at the man on the Chris Craft who stood watching happily through his binoculars.

It was a few minutes before the boys came back, cutting a swath across the quiet bay. And behind them, the porpoises reappeared. They were leaping out of the water, twirling in the air, water drops glittering on their skin. They did flips and cartwheels, landing with great splashes on their back, then rising again with flicks of their tail.

"They like it," Kristin said. "They really like it."

The boys came over in their whaler, their faces flushed and happy. They stopped beside us, and one of the young hellions reached out to shut off the outboard. The other stood up and put his hand on the gunwale.

"Excuse me," he said. "We caught a big codfish this morning. It's way too big for us. My dad was wondering if you'd like half of it. For dinner?"

We looked at each other, a bit guiltily, and thanked them for the fish. "Nice kids," I said, as they puttered off. That evening, with the smell of frying cod drifting through the bay, we listened to the ravens croaking from the trees and watched the otters paddling along the shore.

Fifty feet away, we could see the family in the Chris Craft sitting down to dinner, lights glowing warmly in the windows. They were laughing and talking as they passed plates around the table. And in the darkness, we waved to them. Our only friends for fifty miles around.

Like a Salmon

A FEW DAYS FROM HOME, I STOPPED AT LOWE INLET and rode a rising tide into Nettle Basin. It's like a bowl, with mountains for rims, and the water a wonderful emerald green. *Nid* crawled across it like a beetle over a rain-water pond, and I hurried to the bow to let the anchor go.

The boat snubbed up on the line and turned slowly end for end. The dog, hearing the sounds, knowing the routine, poised herself by the dinghy.

We rowed to a little islet and stretched out on the ground amid long grass and wildflowers. I could hear the waterfall at the head of the basin and, behind me, song birds fluttering through berry bushes. It was my nineteenth day alone. I felt like a salmon, swimming slowly home. I hadn't seen another boat for almost a week, or spoken to anyone but the dog in almost ten days.

I hadn't stopped at Lowe Inlet for more than two years. There'd been a fleet of boats in the basin then, sailboats and powerboats, seiners from Alaska. They were anchored in a long arc on each side of the falls. Only the Alaskans went swimming, leaping from the very tops of their high, roofed-over bridge decks.

Kristin had been with me then. We'd watched from the shore, from the bushes, training binoculars on the anchored boats.

"What's that?" she'd said, and pointed. "That thing in the water there."

It was a dark shape moving among the boats, a brown blob working slowly toward the rocks at the river mouth. When it reached a small powerboat, it stopped, and a man came out of the cabin. He stood peering down at it.

I focused the binoculars. "It's a head," I said. I could see the face, in profile, the wet hair smooth as a helmet. It was one of the Alaskans, off for his swim. We could hear the voices, as the boater leaned on his railing and called down to the disembodied head. They talked about fishing.

"We caught two springs off Humpback," said the boater. His arm went back and forth like a fishing rod. "Bang, bang; right in a row."

And the head said, "Yeah, we're going up to Ketchikan," and then it turned, and bobbed off across the water as though it were already on its way.

Now, two years later, I watched the anchorage fill again. The boats came throughout the afternoon, all big motor yachts with burgees on the bow and American flags on the stern. Again, they made a long arc across the falls, like a rainbow of fiberglass and chrome.

The dog back in the dinghy, I rowed through the fleet to the mouth of the river, passed the first point and drifted into a pool below the waterfall.

In the river current, the water rippled and churned. Flecks of foam came spinning out of the falls. And salmon—scores of salmon—flopped and splashed at the surface, poking their heads up as though to get a better look at the obstacle ahead.

On the rocks beside the waterfall, right in the spray, a big black bear snatched at the fish as they rose thrashing from the rapids and flung themselves at the falling water.

They went zinging past him on each side, bubbling up like lottery balls. They splashed at his feet, soared by his head; they fell, writhing, on the rocks where he stood. And he grabbed at them, clumsy as a clown, rearing up like King Kong swatting at buzzing biplanes.

People in windbreakers came gliding past me in Boston Whalers. Four in a boat, five in a boat, they zigged back and forth, cut in front of me, sat there with the big outboards idling. In the wind of the falls, I smelled gasoline and perfume.

They cheered for the bear. They oohed and aahhed when his paws swept close by a flying salmon. And when he finally caught one and grabbed it in his teeth, they applauded. Then, satisfied, they turned their boats and roared off again across the basin.

It was the salmon that deserved the applause. I stayed for an hour, watching them hurl themselves up the falls, only to be swept back down. In all that time, not one made it over the top. Yet eventually thousands would get up there, only to find another waterfall beyond, ten times as high.

I couldn't understand what drove them so hard, why they couldn't wait for the tide to lift them to the top of the falls. They had an urge to get home; I could understand that. But what if they slowed down, went with the tide and the currents, and took time to rest? Would they still have to die in the end?

Filling the Void

E SAW THE LIGHT STATIONS DISAPPEAR, overnight it seemed. They went like the dinosaurs, suddenly and inexplicably.

We saw Lucy Island burn, a shroud of black smoke clinging to the island and drifting out over Chatham Sound. And where we used to sit with the light keeper and his family, we stood by a chain link fence and watched a wind gauge go round and round.

We saw Pointer Island vanish, like an elephant in a magic trick. There was a light station there when we passed, and a white house trimmed in red. And when we looked again, there was a crumbling ruin and a pile of tortured metal.

"Didn't there used to be a lighthouse there?" Kristin said. In the time it took us to go two hundred miles and back, another light keeper had become extinct.

And now there are more going, like the carrier pigeons and the prairie bison. And on the North Coast, only one will be left. Triple Island will still be there, like a rookery for the last of the Dodo birds.

Oh, I know, Transport Canada will say the automated weather stations work just fine. They'll do everything the lightkeepers do, except save lives. But I

somehow don't believe it. And I bought a "Taylor Five-Way Weather Meter" to fill the coming void.

It came in a box about the size of a large ashtray. "Your personal weather bureau," it says on the back, "provides instant weather reports." It measures rainfall and temperature, wind direction and velocity. It does everything Lucy Island does and more, for only eight dollars and twenty three cents.

I screwed it to a two-by-four hammered into the edge of the garden, attached the Wind Speed Indicator flap and the Graduated Rainfall Tube. I set the sliding rain scale to zero. Then I went inside to watch the coming storm.

The Weather Meter twitched when the first gusts came. It turned a circle to the left and a circle to the right. The wind was coming from everywhere and from nowhere, because the Wind Direction indicator wasn't working very well. It was off by about 45 degrees, due to a malfunction of the two-by-four. But that's to be expected, I think, in these automated weather stations.

The thermometer had plummeted to forty degrees, and I tried to read the bilingual Wind Chill Chart as it spun and quivered in the storm.

By nightfall, when Kristin came back from town, the Taylor Weather Meter was twitching and shaking on its post. The Wind Speed Indicator flap was leaping up and down the scale as the storm gusted to forty knots, then fifty-five. It peaked at sixty knots, and the meter jammed there for a moment.

All night, with the windows slick with rain and buckling in the wind, we could see the Taylor Weather Meter swinging back and forth. And when the gusts went whistling through the eaves, we'd see the Wind Speed Indicator flap pinned in place at sixty knots.

"So this is what Lawyer Island is like now," Kristin said. "I guess everyone's going to keep phoning us, to ask what the weather is."

In the morning, there was half an inch of water in the Graduated Rainfall Tube. The Taylor Weather Meter had settled at a steady 25 knots, and I felt I could cope now with the demise of the lightkeepers.

Sure, it had cost me eight dollars and twenty-three cents. But the way I look at it, what's money really worth, when safety is at stake?

Getting There

I ONCE LIVED IN AN INTERIOR TOWN WHERE THE WIND BLEW HOT through streets as straight as rulers, and whirled the dust into small tornadoes. I worked in a newspaper office that would shake as the trains rumbled by westward to the coast. I sat in a chair that creaked like hemp-rope rigging.

The fellow I worked with had been a sailor at one time. He'd sold his boat to move inland and plow seas of summer hay from the seat of an ancient tractor. And he told me how he'd actually sat down on his bit of land and cried in frustration because his tractor was falling apart and his crops were rotting in the field. One day, he said, he'd sell it all and get a boat again.

We both had similar dreams. He would go to the South Pacific and cruise among the islands there, plucking fruit from the trees, and fish from the sea. He'd sail everywhere, and not bother with an engine at all. And he'd never, ever, look again upon a tractor.

"And where would you be?" he said. "If you could be anywhere in the world?"

A pickup truck clattered past. Dust drifted in through the open window. I leaned back, and the chair creaked.

"I'm in the Black Sea," I said. "I'm anchored off Constanta or the Bosporus, or somewhere in there, and my boat—my ketch," I said, "—is sun-baked and weather beaten. Night's just fallen, and the kerosene lamps are swinging on their hooks;" I said. "They're casting golden shadows through the hatch. There's a Russian girl sprawled on the settee in a thick sweater that comes partway down her thighs. She's reading stories to me," I said, "out of *Pravda*. And she's laughing."

I could smell, for just a moment, the olive trees and cypress in the swirl of road dust from the street below. And there was a taste of salt in there too, from very far away.

My friend went south soon after that, but not as far as he hoped. He bought a house in the city, and started a new career. And I think about him every year at this time, when we start loading the boat for our summer cruise. We've less than a month to go before we're off again on another Gypsy sort of voyage. We don't know exactly where we're going, or just when we'll be back.

"So you don't have firm plans yet," someone said the other day.

"Sure we do," I said. "We're going south." It was the only decision we'd had to make. And though we really had only three choices, we'd agonized over it for weeks.

Already we've got the boat half packed, so it's sitting at a bit of a list against the dock. The house is full of boxes and tubs, and every day or two Kristin comes home with a new paperback for the book supply. Yesterday it was *Voyage of the Dawn Treader*.

"I remember that," I said. It was a favorite from my childhood. I held out my hand, ready to travel again right then back to the Lost Islands and the land of the Dufflepuds.

"No, no," said Kristin. It was her dog-obedience voice. "You can't read that now." She stuffed the book down in the bottom of the box, hiding it under murder mysteries and biology texts, so far down it would take weeks to get to.

"We'll read a little bit of it each night," she said, and closed the carton. "We'll read it aloud."

We're in Fitz Hugh Sound. We're anchored off Namu or Calvert Island, and my boat—it's not as big as I'd hoped—is sun-baked and weather beaten. Night's just fallen, and Kristin is sprawled out on the bunk with the blankets drawn around her. She's reading stories to me, of the Dufflepuds.

And of course she's laughing.

It's not quite my dream but I'm getting there.

A Ritual by Moonlight

MOONLIGHT COMES DOWN THROUGH THE FORWARD HATCH, a beam of weird, silvery light that glows on Kristin's back as she crawls feet first into the berth and disappears behind the bulkhead. The boat tilts, and through the square of Plexiglass the stars slosh back and forth like ball bearings in a blue-black bowl.

This is a ritual, and so it has its ordered steps and progression of rites. Kristin squirms and settles; she fluffs the pillow. She holds the little alarm clock up to the shaft of moonlight, sets it, and then, stretching, places it exactly so on the corner of the chart table.

Her head thumps back; sometimes it cracks on the bulkhead. Always, the covers rustle. "Okay," she says. "Have you got something to read?" The log book, she means. Not the last entry, but every one on this date for all the years we've been sailing.

I sigh; I always do. Then I get out the book and spread it open. I bend the gooseneck lamp close to the page. The handwriting can be hard to read.

"Okay," I say. "Here's what we did a year ago today."

The entries never take long to read. I tell her where we were and which way we were going. And sometimes I have to squint at the page when the writing was done in a hurry, when the words tumble and twist in a frightened stampede.

"Left a couple of hours before low tide, heading out into a stormy passage with southeast winds and large, breaking waves eight to ten feet high. Made no progress to the south, turned north and ran under staysail to the top of Dundas. Anchored in Goose Bay."

"That's it?" says Kristin.

"That's it," I say, and close the book.

She rolls onto her back. "It was an awful storm, wasn't it?"

"It calmed down later," I tell her. We've both slipped back to that day. "We heard the sea lions from Zayas Island."

"And we found all those rock piles in Goose Bay," says Kristin, remembering, with the moonlight on her face. "Wasn't that the place where you made a rope ladder?"

I laugh. "There was rope everywhere. It kept tangling into big heaps."

"I was sleeping."

"And you woke up dreaming of a spaghetti dinner."

Ah yes, we remember it well.

Kristin rolls over. Above her, the stars slosh side to side. "So what were we doing two years ago?"

I sigh again, but I'm already leafing back through the book. Two years ago we were off Namu, charging through fog banks that blew in from the sea. The year before that, on this very day, we were down in Campbell River.

"At Heriot Bay?" asks Kristin. I tell her yes.

"We had a good time, didn't we?" It was hot and sunny, and we had barbecued salmon on the sand at Rebecca Spit.

And now, three years later, we walk again along that strip of beach while the stars roll across the hatch and moonlight comes streaming in.

"Good night," says Kristin.

"Good night," I say.

It's our ritual by moonlight.

Rolling in the Rain

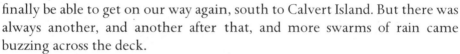

THE WEATHER WAS COLD AND DARK.
Bands of black and inky clouds passed one
after the other, changing as they moved
like spreading stains. They brought
rain in drops the size of horseflies;
huge swarms of them.

We watched each cloud sweeping down and thought this would
be the last one. Behind it would be
clear sky and sunshine, and we'd
finally be able to get on our way again, south to Calvert Island. But there was
always another, and another after that, and more swarms of rain came
buzzing across the deck.

The wind rushed straight at us over the trees, but the swell washed sideways through the channel we'd chosen for a temporary anchorage. Suspended
between two anchors, the boat rocked back and forth like a rolling pin.

We'd already gone cod-jigging in the rain; we snagged the lure on a rocky bottom. We'd already gone beach combing; we brought back a roll of plastic freezer wrap. We could hear the roll wandering across the deck, thudding against
the mast, against the rail, thundering over the cabin top like a loose cannon.

"I don't know why you want that," said Kristin. "What are you going to do
with freezer wrap?"

I shrugged. "Wrap stuff, I guess."

"I really don't think you're going to need to wrap anything in the next few
days."

"You never know," I said, too lazy to go up and get it.

The boat rolled, and the freezer wrap thumped against the mast. Kristin
gritted her teeth. "I wish you'd get rid of that."

"It's fine there," I said, and we glowered at each across the cabin. Our shadows slithered up and down with each roll of the boat. And with each roll I
leaned forward and Kristin leaned back. Bilge water slurped up the planks; the
kettle tilted on its battered bottom, clanging like a bell; the boom creaked to
the left. Then the boat rolled the other way; Kristin leaned forward and I
leaned back, and the boom creaked to the right. Above us, a sheet block
tapped the deck, and tapped again.

"Oh, I hate this weather. This rolling," said Kristin, and looked out to see if the cloud bleeding across the sky was followed yet by sunshine. It wasn't.

Sometimes porpoises came puffing by, but we didn't bother looking anymore, not after two days. And on the third day, when something twittered in the trees, we barely moved at all.

"Was that the laughing cry of the gull?" asked Kristin, leaning forward.

"No," I said. The bilge water sloshed under my seat. "I think it was the haunting call of the loon." We felt better somehow, and chuckled as the kettle tolled on the stove.

That's all it takes sometimes, just a little smile that brightens the gloom like a match flaring in the dark. On that third day, it was enough to stir us up, and get us going. We hauled on our bib-pants, raincoats, and boots and climbed outside. The raindrops were on us in an instant. They pecked at our hands, stung our cheeks. They flew in our eyes and in our mouths. And we swatted at them madly.

The boat rocked and spilled water down the cabin side. The boom scythed across the deck. I tightened the sheet and the creaking stopped.

We took our spare lines and tied them together, three hundred feet of them, to reach a solid tree high on the shore. When we pulled them taut, they snapped from the water like a string of shining beads and the boat turned sideways, across the wind.

Right away, the awful rolling stopped. The kettle fell silent. And when the next swell touched the bow, the boat lifted and fell. It sat there, bobbing quietly, like a seabird dipping its head in the waves.

"Well, that's better," said Kristin. "Let's go back below."

We hung up our clothes and sat in our same spots, facing each other across the cabin. The boat rose on a swell; we both leaned sideways. It dropped in the trough, and we leaned the other way. Above us, the halyards banged on the mast. The anchor line creaked in the roller.

"So," said Kristin, "you think the next cloud is the last one?"

Breaking Loose

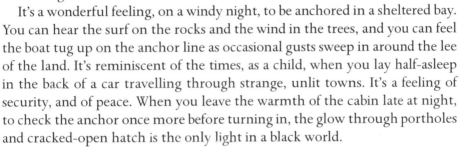

From the shelter of a small cranny in the shore of Grenville Channel we could see grey waves capped with foam. The southeast wind had come up in mid-afternoon, bringing cold rain that made progress down the channel slow and miserable.

We put out a stern anchor to keep us in the center of the little cove, and settled down for the night.

It's a wonderful feeling, on a windy night, to be anchored in a sheltered bay. You can hear the surf on the rocks and the wind in the trees, and you can feel the boat tug up on the anchor line as occasional gusts sweep in around the lee of the land. It's reminiscent of the times, as a child, when you lay half-asleep in the back of a car travelling through strange, unlit towns. It's a feeling of security, and of peace. When you leave the warmth of the cabin late at night, to check the anchor once more before turning in, the glow through portholes and cracked-open hatch is the only light in a black world.

I untied the dinghy from the cleat, let out a bit more anchor line, and snubbed it down. Wet and cold after the few minutes' effort, I fled back into the cabin and slid the hatch shut.

By morning, the wind was gone, and birds sang in the trees as a bright sun burned puddles of rain from the deck. But the dinghy had disappeared. I remembered untying it to adjust the anchor. But I couldn't remember tying it up again afterwards.

I was scanning the shoreline through binoculars when Kristin appeared in the cockpit with lifejacket and oars, holding the canvas sling we used to lower the old dog onto the floor of the inflatable.

"The dinghy's gone," I said, and she peered over the side as though I could have overlooked its black bulk in the water.

"It must have broken loose," I told her, less ashamed of the lie than of my mistake. "It was here when I checked the anchor."

Kristin took it well. She looked out into Grenville Channel where a low swell had replaced the waves that funneled up the passage. "It'll be twenty miles away by now," she said.

We motored along the shore for a while, hoping the inflatable had jammed among the rocks, then turned the corner into Kumealon Inlet where the pilot book said loggers had a barge camp. They lent us a skiff, filled its tiny tank through a massive hose normally used by tugboats.

"I can't understand how this could happen," Kristin said as we searched carefully the beaches of our little bay. I shrugged. "It's probably back in Oona River already," she said.

We found the boat wedged into a cleft in the rocks, and towed it back to the camp where the loggers were waiting for a floatplane that would take them out to Rupert.

I spliced a new towline onto the dinghy, replacing the frayed rope that Kristin blamed for the loss, and I spliced a snaphook onto the end of the line.

"Well that won't break loose again," said the logger who'd given us the skiff. He tried to refuse our payment of a bottle of Lamb's Navy Rum, though not quite hard enough in the end.

Later, when Kristin suggested we bring the dinghy up onto the deck at night, I told her the truth, that I'd forgotten to tie it up the night before. It didn't break loose, I said. It just drifted away.

Confession's good for the soul, I guess. But it doesn't do much for the ego.

Night Sailing

IT'S A SUMMER EVENING, WARM, WITH THE WIND FROM THE WEST. You've been sailing all day, with a reef in the mainsail and the headsails straining, pulling you along.

The boat is heeling over, dipping her decks in the water when she rolls off a wave down into a trough. The staysail flutters, cracks taut again, and the wave hisses under the boat, frothing against the hull. The tip of the boom touches the water, digs a furrow there, and the bow rises over the next wave, tossing spray across the deck. The sails are wet, glistening in the sun.

There's no land to the west for four thousand miles and you watch the sun set over the sea, tinting the jib a dusky rose. You adjust course, turn east, and follow a trail of light across the waves. Just before dark, you take down the staysail and stand on the bow in the twilight, watching the moon rise, as the boat rolls and plunges along.

Stars appear one by one and, then by the hundreds, fill the sky. You can see the shape of the sails against them, but nothing else, and the half-moon makes ghostly shadows on the water.

You steer by the wind, by the feel of it on your face, by the shaking of the sails and the motion of the boat in the waves. Now and again, you shine a dim light on the compass and push the tiller, ever so slightly, one way or another.

There are prickles of phosphorescence in the water where it's thrown back by the bow, where the waves break close by with a sound like whales blowing when they surface. Close under the stern and around the rudder, the water glows emerald green.

You head east. The northern lights ripple across the top of the sky, above the masthead where it corkscrews among the stars. Moonbeams reflect off dripping sails, and you listen to the creak of ropes and the rush of water past the hull. A pale, ragged shape rises from the sea ahead and floats off across the wind when the boat wakes a sleeping gull.

The wind drops, and the seas flatten. There's still a breeze, cold now, and you pull up the collar of your jacket, nestle down behind the cockpit coaming with your arm over the tiller. The hatch cover slides open, you see the yellow flame of a kerosene lamp swinging in the cabin. You're handed a mug of scalding cocoa and you sip it, feel it hot and sweet on your lips.

You pick up the shore lights and steer toward them, haul in the jib sheet a bit, and the main. The boat heels to the wind again, and prances off across coal-black waves.

Close to the channel, you see the lights of fishing boats red and green and white. You turn on your running lights until they pass, see the glow on the sails and water, then turn them off again, to save the battery.

You're sorry when the dawn comes, a pale glimmer in the sky. Soon you can see shapes again, and colors. And then the sun comes up from the hills ahead, and water rises from the deck and sails in tendrils of steam.

You shake the reef out of the main and haul up the staysail from its bundle on the deck. You trim the sheets and feel the boat pick up speed, feel the rudder vibrating in the water.

It's daylight now, and with the darkness goes the magic, with the sunrise comes a harbour.

When the dawn comes, a pale glimmer in the sky

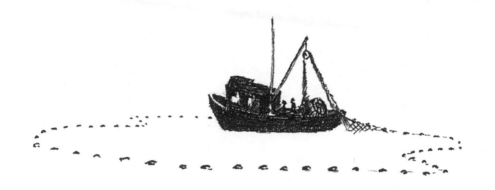

Shoes for the Finding

IT WAS A POPULAR ANCHORAGE ON CALVERT ISLAND, and it filled toward evening with a dozen boats swinging close together on their anchors.

At the end of the day, a fisheries officer came amongst them in an orange Zodiac. He puttered from boat to boat, stopping at each one like a Salvation Army officer canvassing a crowded bar, and paused eventually beside us.

He was wearing mirrored glasses and we could see ourselves reflected there, between the brim of his cap and a thin, humorless mouth.

"Do you have any fish on board?" he asked, and we said no.

We'd spent the day walking for miles on sandy beaches, crossing one headland after another on serpentine trails footprinted by otters and deer.

"Have you done any fishing?" he asked, and we said no again.

We'd seen dead fish on the beach, though. Big cods lying in the sand at the high tide mark. From a distance it looked as though they were moving, their skin rippling. But when we got closer, the layers of flies rose from the bared bones where thick filets had been sliced from both sides.

"Are you planning on fishing?" he asked, and we nodded. In his glasses, we nodded again.

We'd found other things on the beach, too. Net floats and a white mooring fender, jerry cans and bottles marked with Japanese writing. "Is that a bear?" Kristin had asked suddenly, and I'd looked up, startled.

"There, right beside you," she'd said, and I'd started, jumping to my feet, when I saw it in the sand; a little honey pot molded in the shape of a teddy bear.

The fisheries officer stared up at us.

"You've got licenses?" he asked, and we told him yes.

And shoes. We'd found them, one after another, scattered along the beach, tossed up among the driftwood logs. "It looks like a ship went down," I'd said, "and all the soles were lost."

But Kristin hadn't laughed, and I prattled on. "Maybe it collided with a shipload of socks."

They were Nikes, half-buried in the sand and heavily populated with barnacles and mussels. We'd set them on logs at first, and wandered on. But we found matching ones later, collected them all in a pile, and sorted out two pairs.

There were still laces in some of the shoes. Kristin tied her pair and laughed. "I'll bet even the mermaids around here are wearing shoes."

The fisheries officer moved away, his glasses glinting in the sun. I called after him. "Are the abalone still closed?" and he said yes, they were.

"What about shoes?" Kristin asked. "Is it closed for shoes?"

He smiled then, as he drifted off around the bow of the boat. A barge had gone down off the Washington coast, he told us, and there were Nikes scattered from Cape Flattery to Alaska.

"Everyone's finding them," he said.

We found more shoes the next day, and the day after that—a golf shoe in the sand, a child's runner among the rocks.

So neither of us was very surprised when I stepped over a sand dune and found, neatly folded and rolled together, two pairs of white cotton socks.

Getting Started

I LIFT OFF THE ENGINE COVER WITH A SENSE OF FOREBODING. I squirt a few drops of oil into the nipple, tinker more than necessary with the fuel lines and the throttle linkage. I pick up the hand-starting crank and fit it to the tangs on the end of the shaft. I sigh softly.

It was a year ago, exactly, that the heavy metal handle slipped off the shaft. It spun in the air, and sliced through the flesh of my nose, between the nostrils. I staggered back from the engine, my hands flying up to my face, blood gushing out and flowing down my wrists, my chest. Kristin pried apart my hands and pressed her fingers into the blood. The look on her face told me it wasn't just a simple nosebleed. She gave me towels soaked in cool water, and raced up the dock to find a telephone.

I bend over the engine now, a year later, and reach for the decompression lever. I turn the handle backward for a revolution or two, then forward. I feel the clutch slip into place.

There was only one doctor in Kelsey Bay, where engine troubles had left us stranded. Something inside the engine was broken, but we didn't know that. "Just keep turning it," everyone told me. "It'll start. Just keep turning."

The doctor lived not far from the dock, in a house with his office in the basement. We had to enter through the carport, past his furnace and the heating pipes, to get to his waiting room. The walls were yellow with shelves of National Geographic, and a young woman sat on an old grey chesterfield. The doctor came to greet us in Bermuda shorts and carpet slippers.

"I'll look after her first," he said. "It'll take a little longer to sew your nose back onto your face."

I stand at the engine, in a crouch before it. I put my weight on the handle, turning slowly at first. The oil indicator starts to spin. I can hear gears whispering.

The doctor led me into his examining room. I stretched out on a table while he searched through shelves and boxes for cotton swabs, needles and thread. He looked at my nose through one of those magnifying glasses that stamp collectors use. He was the nicest doctor I'd ever met.

"You know," he said, as he set to work with a fistful of syringes, "the loggers,

85

if they cut themselves in the bush, pack their wounds with pine sap. It seems to work. Miners used coal dust the same way."

Smiling, he shoved the needle in through my nose. "I don't know what sailors would do in a case like this," he said. "Immerse their head in a bucket of salt water until the bleeding stopped, I suppose."

I can still hear his laugh as I crank over the engine this morning. Valves whir and pop. The oil indicator flashes red and white on top of the block. The injector spits fuel with a hiss, faster and faster as I turn the handle.

The doctor put two stitches in my face. He gave me a vial of nose medicine and charged me ten dollars. When we walked out of his office it seemed that the whole town knew what had happened. A bush mechanic spent his evenings lying on his stomach above the motor. He found the push rods in a pool of black oil, and a rocker arm fractured in two. The skipper of a charter boat lent us his Jeep to collect a new part from the bus depot at the highway.

The drive chain squeals on its gears now. I watch the handle pass the top, counting revolutions. The decompression lever jogs against my thumb. The fuel pump squirts and the injector hisses. The sounds all run together.

When the mechanic fixed the motor, we danced along the dock. And still he stayed, adjusting things, setting valves and timing. The motor had never sounded as good as it did when he finally finished. We slipped out of Kelsey Bay with the next tide, early in the morning. There was no one on the dock to wave goodbye, but we knew we were leaving friends behind.

I release the lever and feel the engine work, air compressing. I drive the handle round, and the engine coughs. Around again and I hear it thump and shudder. It catches up, then overtakes me. I pull the throttle back to a slow idle.

Again, I've got it started. It's all in the wrist, and the nose.

Lying Beside Corrine

SHE WAS OLD AND BATTERED, and her planks were riddled with holes. And one calm, summer day, *Corrine* went to Davy Jones.

It was a short trip, though, for the water was shallow close to shore. So they raised her up, and pumped her out, and hauled her off to the little shipyard across the bay. One of her hatch covers was missing, the wheelhouse door was gone, and a few pieces of planking came adrift and floated off. But those were minor things.

We saw her, leaning for support against the dock, when we came into Shearwater for engine repairs. She was painted a sickly, toothpaste green, and there was a big chunk missing from one side. Her decks were riddled with little holes, like a scattering of shotgun pellets on a deer-crossing sign. You could stand there at the edge of the dock, with *Corrine* leaning under your feet, and watch the water rising in her hull.

A "ratty old gillnetter," the shipyard boss called her. He looked at us and said: "Tie up beside that ratty old gillnetter."

So we lay beside *Corrine*. And someone came down with a sump pump and lowered it into her bilge. He watched the water bubbling up for a moment, and smiled. She wasn't leaking nearly so badly any more, he said.

It was crowded at the shipyard, so at first we didn't mind lying beside *Corrine* like that. They put a brand new bilge pump down in her hold, and all

night we heard the gurgle and gush of water against the boat. It was sort of pleasant and idyllic, as though we were anchored off a little waterfall somewhere.

But in the morning there was a great slick of oil all around us, and *Corrine* was going down for the second time.

They came with a battery charger then, and hooked it up to the pump. We sat and listened to the rush of water, and watched *Corrine* rise slowly beside us.

There were advantages in lying beside *Corrine* that way. We could air our bedding on her davits, and hang a sail to dry on her wheelhouse roof. And when an extension cord from shore was too short to reach over her decks, I just poked a hole in one of her planks with my thumb and passed it through there.

And still we lay beside *Corrine*. We were bound together like Siamese twins, and the shipyard moved us both up and down the dock as other boats came and went. We weren't a big priority at the little yard.

She went down for the third time late one night. The boss himself came in his dress pants and crawled around in her oily bilge to replace the pump that had burned out from over-use. And she went up in the water again, like a frail old lady in a hospital bed.

People walked by and made jokes about *Corrine*, and how they might fix her up for the charter business. A lot of them asked if we weren't taking a bit of a chance, lying beside her like that. And bit by bit, the story of her sinking started to fill in.

She'd been tied to the dock, they said, the day she first went down. The owner had left his dog to watch over *Corrine* while he went to shore. He'd heard it barking, and yelled down to it to shut up. The dog, they said, had stood on the bow as *Corrine* went down.

For fourteen days we lay beside *Corrine*. Then we slipped away from her, our untied lines trailing in the water to wash the oil away. We anchored that night as far as possible from the little shipyard, and scrubbed the scum from the sides of the boat.

There were long smears, like handprints, running high above the water line. She'd been clinging to us, I think, hanging on for dear life as we lay beside *Corrine*.

The Little People

KRISTIN CALLS THEM THE LITTLE PEOPLE. We didn't even know they existed until this year, though there's a whole community of them out there, on the water.

They travel by day, close to the land. At night, the little people come ashore, haul their frail wee boats up on the beach, and light cooking fires with driftwood and bits of bark.

We travelled hundreds of miles along the coast, for days and weeks at a time, before we met the little people for the first time at Oona River. They came around the point in a steamy calm, the hills behind them obscured in a morning mist. Their open boats were long and sleek, driven by oars that rested in delicate frames extending beyond the gunwales.

We met more near Bella Bella, and came across unmistakable signs of them at Namu.

They're friendly folk, the little people. Two of them, voyaging far from home in an open boat less than fifteen feet long, told us they used to wave at every cabin cruiser they saw, but the only people who ever waved back were lost and needed rescuing.

They'll gladly let you look inside their small boats, their canoes and kayaks and sailing skiffs. They'll spend hours telling you of their travels and adventures. And they'll all talk about the elderly lady, legendary among the little people, who travels every year, all by herself, from Vancouver Island to Alaska in a tiny kayak.

"She's a gourmet cook," the rowers told us.

"She has all these incredible, fancy meals packaged up. And for each one there's something to go with it. She might eat Japanese food, and there'll be a little bottle of saki."

Near Bella Bella, the eyes of a European kayaker gleamed when we mentioned the elderly lady. He'd run across her more than once in his eighteen months of paddling. He spoke enthusiastically of her fine meals—a rare break to his usual diet of rice and beans—and of her little bottles of wine and liquor.

"Just a few sips," he said. "When I drink, I like to put a few away. But it was very nice. Just a few sips."

And he spoke of her stamina.

"She's just a little lady. But she goes all by herself," he said. "She left Prince Rupert about the same time as a group of commandos, but they flipped their kayaks in Dixon Entrance and had to abandon their trip. The waves were only four feet, too. It was nearly calm."

"And she made it all the way to Wrangell?" he asked us. "That's good. That's very good."

We left the kayaker on shore as we headed south. He started inland to pick huckleberries to supplement his meagre diet.

With the nights growing cold and the first frost not far off, the men and women in the open boats were heading home. He was the last we'd see—the last of the little people.

A Place Twice Abandoned

IT'S A LONG, SHALLOW BAY, WITH A GAP TO THE WEST between the islands, looking out on the open sea. The land is rocky, glowing gold with seaweed. And the wind comes over the trees, funnelling down through olive-green hills to moan and whine in the rigging.

We rowed ashore to a strip of beach, coarse and white, with broken shells thick as sand. We tied the dinghy to a storm-stripped cedar and picked gooseberries from a bush growing wild along the beach.

Above, almost hidden by masses of bushes and waving grass, the beams and poles of an Indian longhouse lie in a tangled heap.

It's a dark, silent place, though that day the sun was high and the sky filled with gulls and crows; a lonely place, though boats passed steadily through the entrance and gathered in the bay.

The beams are huge and white as bones, scored by adze marks down their lengths like the scales of a fish. They lean at odd angles, this way and that, the way fingers lie on folded hands. Two of the posts have heads carved at the tops; they are fallen now with the faces buried in the forest floor. They have been there for a long, long time.

We stepped among them and between them, and bent down to look underneath. Below the caved-in floor, in a hollow in the ground, lay an old bed frame, its springs stiff and brown and brittle-thin. It seemed incongruous to us, as though it had been mislaid from some other time and place.

It is a place twice abandoned. Sixty years earlier, people had settled on the ruins of an Indian village. They'd built houses roofed with cedar shakes. They'd planted gooseberry bushes, and rowed thirty miles down the coast to sell the berries in the nearest town.

We found their houses deeper in the bush, flat as wads of sodden paper, the frames black with rot, the shakes as thin and white as soda crackers. The ground around them is strewn with old nails and bits of tarred roofing paper. In a few more years, there'll be nothing left at all.

It is a cold place, where the morning fog makes smoke rings through the trees, as it has for a thousand years.

On the island, among the bleached cedars, the skeletons rest in wooden boxes. They lie on the ground, in beds of twigs and moss, peacefully it seems. They nestle in the crooks of tall branches, the boxes greying and draped with tattered beards of green. The trees creak and sway in the wind, and the fog swirls by in breath-like wisps.

And the boxes rock. Gentle as cradles.

It is a place like none we've ever seen. It is a place where time has stopped, preserved like fading pictures in a family album, where nothing at all changes any more. Except for the people who come to see it.

On the Track of the Wildman

OFF THE NORTHERN END OF VANCOUVER ISLAND, not far from Port Hardy, lies a cluster of small islands fringed by rocks and reefs. They say a wildman lives there, an ape-like creature who stalks through the forest and howls at the moon on summer nights.

We listened for him when we were there, anchored at a safe distance from the shore. We might have heard twigs cracking as he passed through the bush, pebbles crunching as he stepped to the water's edge on leathery feet. We might have seen his figure, pale against the darkness of the trees. Or maybe we didn't, for that's how stories get started.

They say the wildman is covered with shaggy hair, with a high, crested head and arms that droop low toward the ground. They say he hunts deer on narrow paths through the bush, or tears mussels from the rocks and eats them shells and all.

I looked for him again from the fantail of the *Queen of the North,* peering through the gloom of a pre-dawn fog with the railing icy against my palms. It was cold on that winter morning, and I huddled in the shelter of a doorway, the deck vibrating under my feet.

I was watching the shore pass close alongside, searching for a sign of the wildman on the beach, when the door crashed open and someone came walking up behind me.

He was a seafaring man, I could tell. He rolled when he walked, reeling from side to side though the ship was steady in the water. His face was red and whiskered, and his hands were thrust into pockets of a parka.

He staggered up to the rail and leaned against it, poking his head over the side to stare forward and then back.

"Where the hell's Alert Bay?" he roared. "We haven't passed it, have we?"

I told him it was up ahead, another thirty miles away.

"On the other side of Hardy, is it?" he shouted, as though calling to me across a hurricane wind. "I fished around here for twenty years but I can't keep all the places straight."

He stared down at the water churning past the hull, then spat over the side and watched until it hit the surface.

"Did you ever hear of the wildman that's supposed to live here?" I said. He grunted, then lurched sideways as though the deck had pitched out from under him.

"I never believed in those stories," he said. "Like them newspapers at the Safeway store about UFOs and people with two heads. You'd have to be crazy to believe that stuff."

I looked at the shore. The sky was yellowing, brightening, and the wildman's islands were slipping away. "I guess so," I said.

"Of course," he said, "there could be some sort of ape man up in the Himalayas or something like that. Somewhere out of the way. That's probably true."

He spat over the side again, then pushed himself from the rail and swayed off across the deck.

I looked back at the islands, dark against the sky, and I might have heard a low cry coming across the water. Birds, probably. Yes, only birds.

Elephants and Sleeping Indians

A SLEEPING INDIAN GUARDS PRINCE RUPERT HARBOUR. He stretches out across the skyline, his head turned toward the zenith. His features are the crags and cliffs of Mount Hays, his headdress a crown of trees. He looms above the Ridley Island superport as you come in from the sea, a welcoming figure visible for miles away.

A fisherman told me about him. He told me to watch for the sleeping Indian, and I looked for him each time I came in from Chatham Sound.

I saw the sleeping Indian once, lying on his back, soaking up the sun and dabbling his feet in the ocean. The next time I passed, I saw only an enormous head looking serenely to the west. And the last time I passed by there, he was nowhere at all to be seen.

The truth is, I don't know if I ever did see the sleeping Indian. But then I've never been very good at picking out those famous figures in the terrain.

Even the Man in the Moon is a stranger to me, though I remember my father trying to point out his features one night when I was very young. We were standing on the back steps of our house looking up at a full moon, when he showed my brother and me the man's cratered eyes and moonscape face.

I held a pair of heavy German binoculars in my hands and raised them to the night sky. I couldn't even see the moon, let alone the little man on top of it. All I saw, as the binoculars weaved about in my hands, were countless stars, all moving in incredible circular patterns.

"Oh," I said. "Shooting stars." My brother hooted with laughter.

This summer, I searched for the head of an enormous elephant that supposedly peers down from the mountains at travellers on the Inside Passage. We were heading south down the east side of Banks Island when I found mention of it in the B.C. pilot book.

"Elephant Head Mountain, a bold cliff face," I read to Kristin. "It resembles the head of an elephant." We looked up and scanned the hills of Pitt Island.

There on the landscape, staring back at us, was a giant beagle. It lay on its stomach atop the most prominent hills with its legs splayed out and its chin resting on the ground. Its floppy ears tumbled down toward us.

But a couple of miles down the channel, the beagle suddenly transformed itself into an elephant. Its long ears became a trunk and its hunched shoulders turned into an elephant's forehead.

Kristin wasn't convinced. She squinted at it, and frowned. "I don't know," she said.

I picked out a couple more elephants in the next few minutes, and had located a small herd of them in the hills before we slipped into Harwood Bay for the night.

We didn't see the real elephant that day, which wasn't surprising after we reread its description in the pilot book again and found the key phrase, "when viewed from Fraser Reach." We'd been looking not only in the wrong direction but at the wrong island altogether.

Weeks later, when we were heading home from up Fraser Reach, we forgot to look for the elephant until it was too late to see anything except the backside of the mountain. And, when we sailed past Ridley Island a few days afterward, we forgot to look for the sleeping Indian, too.

But a few days ago, when the moon was full, I was out on the porch again, looking up and hoping to see the Man in the Moon.

Father and Sons

FOR FIVE DAYS, THE RAIN HAMMERS DOWN. It patters on the cabin top and drips off the sails, gurgles through the scuppers and plops, plops through the little crack in the hatch coaming.

It's like living inside the snare drum of a military marching band. I sit on one side of the boat, my brother on the other. Skipper the dog lies on the bunk, peering woefully at us through her hair.

Once in a while, one of us pushes open the hatch and looks up at the sky. We note which way the clouds are moving, because we can't tell the wind direction in this small, rock-bound, bug-infested bay.

"Still going north," we say, and pull the hatch shut again. We're waiting for the weather to change. There's a warm front coming in, and northerly winds to push us south at a clip.

"Are you sorry you came?" I ask my brother.

"Not yet," he says, and smiles.

"Do you want a book to read?" And he tells me he's brought one along, though he hasn't read it yet.

"What is it?" I laugh, and guess the title. "Technical Aspects of Brushstrokes in Modern Art?"

He smiles again, in a way that looks familiar. "It's called *Nature and the Americans: Three Centuries of Changing Attitudes.* And it's quite good."

"You're just like Dad," I say. "That's what Dad would bring." And when he smiles, again, I know why it looks so familiar. I've seen the same expression a thousand times on my father's face. He'll smile just like that—with the corners of his mouth lifting and his eyes twinkling, squinting—when we tease him about something. Like the budgie he had as a boy and took outside with a bit of string tied to its leg.

We go for short walks along the rocky beach, row out to the mouth of the bay to see if the whitecaps are still rolling up the channel. When we come

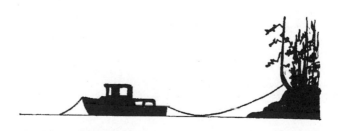

back, shedding layers of rain gear, we watch Skipper to see whose sleeping bag she'll settle on.

"No, Skipper," Donald shouts. "The blue one is warmer. And more absorbent."

Donald leafs through the pilot book, scans the tide tables, thumbs through magazines.

"Here's a picture of Dad's father's boat," he says, holding up a page from *Wooden Boat* with a dozen pictures of a dozen different steam-powered launches.

"Every time he sees a steamboat he says, 'Oh, that's just like my father's.' It doesn't matter what they look like."

Early on the sixth morning, I push open the hatch and the rain has stopped. The clouds are going south, and the sky to the west is bright and blue. We lash the anchor to the bowsprit and head south.

Donald has a ferry to catch at Bella Bella, and we've got a long way to go. For two days and two nights we sail on, putting in a reef at dusk and shaking it out again with the dawn.

The boat seems empty after he's gone. I turn on the radio, to fill the silence, and they're talking about Father's Day on the CBC.

I call home that night on the radio and my father answers. He asks how the trip is going, and says how much he's longed to be with us.

"But you were, Dad," I want to tell him. "But you were."

The Law of the Sea

WE'D AGED THE WINE FOR TWO WEEKS. Lying on its side deep in the bilge, it was getting older and better as we travelled north up the coast. Nine weeks we'd been gone, and we were just one day from home.

I was looking forward to anchoring. For days I'd been planning this. We'd spend the night in a favorite spot in Lawson Harbour, with its beach of gravel the dog loved so much. We'd break out the bottle and pull out the cork and, as the sun went down on our last day at sea, we'd sit and talk of our voyage.

It hadn't been great. Two whole weeks had passed tied to a shipyard dock; we'd spent all we had on engine repairs. Our last money—a handful of quarters and dimes—had gone for the bottle of wine. We had less than a gallon of diesel fuel and not a drop of motor oil; our batteries were dead and we had no way to charge them. We were down to our last tins of food. The rum bottle was empty.

But, when we opened the wine, all that would be forgotten with the pop of the cork. We'd be left with a sunset, and a few hours of sailing to get home.

We trolled round Comrie Head and past the mouth of Alpha Creek. I wanted a barbecue on our last night, a big slab of salmon cooked on the beach. As we puttered along, a big schooner went by and Kristin said, "We should have stopped her and asked for fuel and rum."

I said, "Why would they give us fuel and rum?"

Kristin shrugged. "It's the law of the sea."

We didn't catch a salmon. "That's all right," said Kristin. "I was looking forward to lentils." So we motored up Ogden Channel and, in the evening, turned north into a cold wind and a choppy sea. Then everything went horribly wrong.

The tide was against us. The wind was against us. The boat crashed through the swell, icy spray flew up from the bow, and we rolled and bucked at a speed of a knot and a half. Down in the bilge, the bottle of wine rumbled across the planks, tapping with a chink on the frames.

"When are we going to drink the wine?" asked Kristin.

"When we anchor," I said. It was the first she'd heard of my plan for the night. I should have told her sooner, I know that now. But she hadn't told me of her idea either: to press on to Humpback Bay, to lessen the distance to home. Every night for a week she'd got out the dividers and measured the miles that remained.

Now she sat in the companionway, sheltered from the spray. "Where are you thinking of anchoring tonight?"

"Lawson Harbour."

"What about Humpback Bay?"

"Too far," I said. It was another six miles, another four hours at the speed we were going.

She looked at her watch, studied the chart, and looked at her watch again. She wanted to visit friends at the old cannery. I didn't want to see anyone.

"Let's have a glass of wine," she said.

"No."

"I'll heat it up. We'll feel better then."

"No," I said.

"Why are you being like this?"

I couldn't tell her. My plan sounded silly, even embarrassing, with its notions of romance. And by now I was wet, cold, and irritated. When we passed the last of the reef, I aimed the boat for Lawson Harbour. Then I stood up to watch for rocks. Though we'd entered it once before, it fell in a gap between our charts.

"We shouldn't be going in here," said Kristin. "We don't have charts. We don't have a clue what it's like."

"We do have a clue," I said. "We've been in there before."

"Then go," she snapped, her back filling the hatchway.

So I turned away from Lawson Harbour and continued on against the chop and the spray. I looked at the chart and found another anchorage a mile or two farther on. It was a deep bay, open to the north, but I expected the winds would ease as sunset approached.

"Do you think it's sheltered in there?" asked Kristin.

"I don't know," I said. "I'm just going to go in and see."

"It doesn't look like it would be," she said. "The wind goes right in there." She picked up the chart and pointed to a spot on Smith Island, miles out of our way. "What about here?"

I said, "We could go there, I guess."

Kristin looked at it again. "Isn't that the place we found so horrible?"

"Horrible?"

"Where we found the bear skeleton? The tide was so strong and big trees kept bumping into us?"

"No," I said. "That happened here." I pointed to the south shore of Kennedy Island, where a whole tree—washed down from the river—had rammed into our hull on the falling tide. "We found the skeleton at Smith Island, but that place wasn't horrible."

"Why don't we just go to Humpback Bay?" she said.

I snatched up the chart, determined to continue on to Prince Rupert, though we'd arrive well after dark. But when I thought of entering the harbour without running lights or a radio, I abandoned the idea.

"Where are we going?" asked Kristin.

I almost snarled. "Humpback Bay." And we headed toward the setting sun in a grim and awful mood.

It was almost dark when we finally stopped at Humpback Bay. I rowed out to set the stern anchor and, when I got back to the boat, I had to thrash my way into the cabin, the air was so thick with anger and silence. Kristin had set out the bottle of wine, beside it a cup with no handle and a canning jar without a lid. We were low on glasses.

I opened the bottle and poured out the wine. I nudged the cup an inch toward her, then snatched up the jar. "I'm taking the dog to the beach," I said.

She didn't look up. "Who's going to make dinner?"

"I don't care."

"You will, then."

I rowed to an island and tied the dinghy to a lump of rock. Perched on a log, I watched the sunset turn to night. The familiar islands of Chatham Sound paled against the horizon and disappeared, one by one. The sea calmed and lapped quietly against the shore. The *Queen of the North* slipped by on her way to Prince Rupert, windows lit up like a hotel, topped by a single red running light. She'd be in Prince Rupert within two hours. The next night, we'd be there as well. I knew what I'd do then. I'd fill the fuel and water tanks, call to the dog, and head off alone across the horizon.

In the morning Kristin and I still hadn't spoken. Not a full sentence. I hand-cranked the motor, and we started for home. We crossed a leaden sea under a leaden sky. Green smudges of land floated like blimps where the horizon should have been. A flight of geese crossed above us in a huge, squawking V. The pattern rippled and changed, breaking apart, forming again.

Kristin trained the binoculars on them. "Lots of geese," she said.

"Yes," I said.

"There must be two hundred." They passed each other, long lines snaking across the sky as if they didn't know who was in charge.

We crossed the harbour limit, a row of dots along the chart. After sixty-four days, we were home again. Kristin took out the wine; the bottle was only half empty. She filled up the jar and the cup without a handle. She passed me the jar.

"Here's to the voyage," she said. We clinked the jar against the cup, and we both took a sip. "The trip wasn't really so bad."

I never did head off across the horizon. Seven years later we're still together, and we still go sailing in the summer. But now we have a new ritual. Kristin gets off in Bella Bella and goes home on the ferry, and I spend two weeks alone. That way we never break the rule we learned over a bottle of wine: never end a voyage in anger.

It's *our* law of the sea.

For Old Time's Sake

I SAW AN OLD FRIEND LEAVING TOWN THE OTHER DAY. She was sitting beside the road, looking sad and forlorn, just sitting and waiting to go. From across the street I saw her, and very nearly passed her by.

Once I'd known her well. She'd been mine, if it's all right to say such a thing. I'd ogled her as she lay stretched on a summer beach, and I'd touched every inch of her, rubbed her with oil when she peeled in the sun. I'd seen her go running, wild as the wind, whirling and spinning and prancing along. I'd known her faults, and worried about them as though they were mine.

Six years ago? Was it really that long?

We had sailed together. Through one long summer it was all that we did, in the daytime. We floated in blistering calms, we scudded like clouds before furious winds. We sometimes stayed out until sunset, when darkness sent us hurrying home. But we always stayed in the harbour; she didn't feel safe far from land.

I looked at her, across a road impossibly wide, and I remembered all that.

"Each ship is a little world for the men aboard, a planet that orbits the oceans."

There was a new fellow with her, a stranger to me. If once she was mine, surely now she was his. He hovered over her, flitted around her, like a hummingbird at a flower. They were just starting out with a long way to go; he was doing everything possible to assure that she'd be happy.

It would be easy to keep passing, to pretend that I hadn't seen her. But I couldn't let her go as easily as that. The truth was, I didn't know until then how much I'd cared for her once. I had to meet this fellow who would take her away. And, once more, I had to touch her. For old time's sake.

I crossed the street. It was a very long walk. And I went not to him, but to her.

Sadly, I saw that she'd changed. She seemed smaller than I remembered, more fragile. But of course she was older now; she'd suffered a bit. She had wounds now that she didn't have before. But they were surface scars, and underneath them, as she sat by the road, I could see she was just as sturdy and brave as in that wonderful summer.

The fellow watched me; I knew he would. He watched me reach out a hand and touch my old friend. He watched me caress her.

It surprised me; she felt just the same.

This fellow wasn't the person that I'd watched her go off with four years before. I had to find out where she'd been.

The fellow seemed uncomfortable now. Something had to be said. So I patted my friend for one last time, and turned to this fellow who had taken my place.

I told him, "I used to own this boat."

A Different World

WE WERE SAD TO SEE THE STORM CLOUDS COME SWEEPING IN, to see the ocean change from speckled calm to a brooding green. For two days we'd lounged on little pocket beaches, entrenched in the sand like butter clams.

We'd grown tired of the inside channels and hurried down the outer coast in a gale of wind, with the boat singing as she does, in a voice of rope and stretched rigging. We'd ridden a breaking sea toward this place, our favorite spot, with its patches of white sand at the edge of a continent.

And then the clouds came, in dark bands with silvered edges, like scythes swinging across the sea. Our sunshine turned to shadow. "We should move the boat," said Kristin, "before it gets too stormy."

"Yes," I said. And we went inland. We didn't go far—not more than a mile or two—but we entered a different world where the shore was rock instead of sand, and the trees, no longer gnarled and windblown, were rigid as rows of cage bars. It seemed gloomy at first, hemming us in.

A fat loon swam crying past the boat before we even had the anchor down. Beside us sat two eagles, shredding a pale carcass on a slab of stone. Ravens watched them from the tree limbs. Huge sandhill cranes, always in pairs, flew across the bay wingtip to wingtip like honeymoon couples. They hooted and trumpeted from a patch of grass beyond our bay, and when we rowed off to see them, a shivering mink thrust his head up from the rocks and studied us, his nose twitching, until we'd passed.

When the rain started, we lit the heater and made a tent of tarps along the

boom. We closed in half the boat to keep the wind from coming in. But still we kept poking our heads through the tarps to watch otters playing behind the boat, and the ravens ahead, plotting to outwit the eagles and claim the scraps of rotted fish.

The wind flurried around the mouth of our bay and whipped the channel to foamy whitecaps. We scudded right to its head in the rubber dinghy, our oars spread like studding sails, and tramped up a creek bed to a quiet lake, beaver-dammed in a drowning forest. We climbed over the walls of ancient fish traps and followed wolf trails high in the hills around us.

In the morning, the rain had stopped. A double rainbow formed above the boat, its arc high above the masthead. We could see its end—or its beginning—shimmering red and purple and blue among the trees where the grey-winged cranes sheltered from the rain. We opened the tarps, peeling them back like grape skins, and the forest came alive with songbirds.

"You want to go back to the outer beaches?" I asked.

"No," said Kristin. "I'm sort of tired of the sun. All that heat." I nodded. We settled back against the cockpit coaming and pulled our knees up to our chests. And we watched the eagles looking on as the ravens dined.

It wasn't so bad being inland after all. It was a different sort of world.

Standing at the Edge

A T THE MOUTH OF PRINCE RUPERT HARBOUR, the freighters load at the Fairview Dock. From a small boat passing by, it looks like a concrete cliff, a long grey wall plastered with barnacles, hung with gigantic fenders in staggered rows.

Along the top, the bollards are painted yellow. They poke over the edge like blonde heads, streaming tresses of dribbled paint. Below the bollards and above the barnacles, the dock is covered with graffiti.

The names of ships are painted on the concrete: "Hoegh Musketeer" in bright safety orange; "Sanko Defiant" in rust-colored red. There are other things too: "Babes 'The Cure' Ala" scrawled along the top rail; "TOOT'sie" in bright, sunny yellow. There's even a round happy-face painted in crimson with slanting, Oriental eyes.

It's modern scrimshaw done with brushes and spraycans, the work of sailors who lean out from the decks of their ships, over a gulf of dark water, and leave something behind to show they were there—at the edge of the sea and the land.

In old photographs of the city, the docks are forever full of people—rows of men dressed like undertakers, the ladies at the back, blurs of boys who couldn't stand still for an eighteenth of a second. On the old Ocean Dock, on the steamship wharf, on miles of planks, huge crowds trample on their own shadows.

If you stare long enough at one of these pictures, you can almost imagine the people are moving. You know they will jump when the blast of the ship's whistle startles them. You know they'll watch with serious faces as the lines are cast off the bollards and hauled like snakes aboard the ship. The crowd will move forward then—every man, woman, and boy surging right to the edge, to the last inch of land. They will stay there until the ship disappears down the harbour.

And you know what they're thinking, these people in the old photograph. It's the same feeling you had as a child watching a parade vanish down the street, seeing the clowns and the bands and the horses slip away, wondering where they'd go and if they'd ever stop at all. You watch a ship cast off, and part of you goes with it.

I used to watch these scenes from the Ocean Dock, from the rickety pier of the old grain elevator. The ships I watched were bigger than those in the photographs, and the crowds were smaller. But still there were always a few people there to watch a ship cast off.

Not any more. Today the ships come and go behind railway tracks and barbed wire. And it's a sad port where you can't watch the ships at work, to see how big they really are, how clumsy they've become. Tugboats that seem enormous when you see them alone shrink against their hulls, bustling back and forth like little boys who move an elephant by poking it with sticks. But you can watch it only from a distance.

On a still night, I hear the voices that drift up from the water, speakers and wires turning men to machines. The voices whistle and squawk.

And across the channel, behind the trees, a ship casts off from the superport and heads away to sea. I watch it pass below, a black shape slipping through the forest. A green light ghosting along, a white one that grows fainter and dimmer until it's lost in the darkness of the sea.

Each ship is a little world for the men aboard, a planet that orbits the oceans. Wherever it touches the land, the sailors leave their scrimshaw. And they take part of me with them.

Traffic on Hand

K RISTIN CALLS IT THE SOAPS. "Turn on the soaps," she says, when we're anchored at night and the boat rocks as she crawls into bed. Sometimes she calls it the talking channel. "Is there anything on that stupid talking channel?"

She means the ship-to-shore channel on radio-telephone. Eavesdropping on a party line.

I tune the radio to Noble Mountain or Calvert Island, to Swindle or Trutch. It doesn't matter where we are; the calls are all the same. A man on a boat, and a woman at home. And the conversation is either full of laughter and innuendo or of silences and pain.

For fishermen and pleasure boats, for just about anyone on an isolated coast, it's the only link to family and shore. But it's more than that. When you haven't seen another boat for days, when you haven't talked to a single soul for a fortnight or more, it's comforting to hear another voice, to know you're not alone.

For two years we listened to the soaps from eight to nine. "My mother might call," said Kristin, who'd set up this schedule in case of emergency. She worried about her mother, who was growing old, and worried as well that her mother might worry. And so we sat, and listened.

We heard a man call one woman after another, in rotation, night after night. None of the women knew about the others, and the calls were cold and frosty, full of questions answered by silence, full of worries and anger and doubt. We heard a boy call his father, mid-way through his first trip on a fish-boat. We heard the pride in the father's voice, his embarrassed "good fishing!" at the end of the contact. He couldn't tell his boy he loved him—maybe he wished he could—with a whole fleet tuning in.

But whenever the radio fell into silence and an operator announced incoming traffic, Kristin sat tense and still. It was like a phone ringing at three in the morning. If the call ever came, it wouldn't be good news; it would have to be bad.

After two years of tuning in to the soaps, we'd heard enough. It seemed too sad to listen, too private and sad.

This year, before we left, my father asked me: "How can I call you? When do you monitor your radio?"

"We don't," I said.

He sighed. I could picture him frowning into the phone. "Why not?" he asked.

"Because no one ever calls."

Then one day we came out from the channels, out from the mountains to the open coast, where for the first time in a week we could receive the Coast Guard weather on the radio. At the end, the announcer said there was traffic on hand for the *Nid*.

Kristin was steering. I shut off the radio and went up on deck. "The Coast Guard has a message for us," I told her.

She looked up, a smile fading, and we stared at each other in awful anticipation. "You'd better call them," she said.

It was a dreadful thought; I wanted the message to be for Kristin but it was for me. "Call home."

The operator at Swindle Island was chatty and pleasant; they always are on the radio-telephone. I gave her the number and she put me through.

My Dad answered. His voice sounded old and worried. I thought of Mom, and the moment it took him to speak seemed very long. Finally, he said, "Thank goodness! We've been trying for days to get hold of you."

"I'm sorry," I said. "Is anything wrong?"

"No, everything's fine. We worry about you, you know."

Salps at Sea

THEY SEEMED TO SWARM AROUND THE BOAT
late in the summer, creatures we'd never
seen before. Weird things with thin, transparent bodies.

"What ARE those?" we asked as they drifted by like ghost fish.

And north of McInnes, we met a thousand of them. It was a rocky, lonely spot where the surf pounds forever on off-lying rocks, where islands of splintered rock are worn as smooth as whale backs on the side fronting the sea. Behind the rocks is a bay, a broad lagoon, where you sit on a placid sea. You hear the surf and the wind, the cries of the gulls, and the mournful, monotonous tolling of the bell at Jaffrey Rock.

It's daunting, going in there. Even the boat seems to quiver; its little heart of a motor runs with a faltering beat.

We passed the first rocks, entered the maze; and the creatures came. They were the size and shape of the cuttlefish bones I'd once fed as a child to a budgie named Joey, jamming them in through the bars of his cage. But I'd never wanted to ask what bird toys looked like when they were still swimming through the seas.

I peered over the side. They bumped against the planks, these things; they swirled in the propeller wash. I dipped at them with a bucket, but they went churning from its mouth.

"Watch the rocks!" cried Kristin. And we went through the channel like a bagatelle ball, from rock to rock as I stared at those things. But when we anchored, we had one in a bucket.

It was hard and slimy, like the too-solid Jello we'd made with tepid creek water, but clear as an ice cube. It had an eye at one end, an egg-yolk ooze of intestines and organs, a slender tube running straight to the tail. Barnacles look something like this, in their wild days of youth, before they glue their heads to the rocks and settle down in their shells, their houses, their tombs. But these would be monster barnacles, big as sewer rats.

"It's dead," I said, poking it.

"I know," said Kristin. "They all are. Dead or dying." She was right. They were breaking apart, rotting in the water, moseying along in a huge dead herd.

Two months later, I looked up from a magazine and asked her: "Have you ever heard of a salp?" I read her the description—"like a tadpole . . . a blob of gelatin." We looked at the picture, and there was our creature.

Some strange current had brought the salps up from the tropics, from a warm-water place where they'd fed on plankton in the surface sunshine.

I said, "They're in the same phylum as man. They're related to us." It seemed amazing, but their thin cords were spines, backbones, holding networks of nerves. They had drifted thousands of miles, knowing that something was wrong, feeling the water change from warm to cool to icy-cold. One by one, and then by scores, they died on an alien shore.

Summer in a Jar

When Kristin pries the lid off the canning jar, a bit of air comes rushing out, sweet as a summer breeze. It carries the smell of Kynumpt Harbour, where we picked the blackberries that Kristin turns to jam.

She spreads a spoonful on French toast and, with snow falling on a wintry morning, we slip back to memories of one summer.

"It must have been the first year we were there," she says. Across the brass top, she had written the name of the harbour, and the date. "Remember how thick the berries were?"

I remember she hadn't wanted to stop there at all. We'd left Lizzie Cove that morning and she wanted to reach Ivory Island before dark. We were heading home, so Kristin was in a hurry; I wasn't.

As we passed Dryad Point, the westerlies were blowing straight up Seaforth Channel. I saw the harbour open up and said, "Let's stop here." Kristin said, "We'll never get home if we keep making short little trips."

I remember thinking the same thing myself but I didn't say anything.

She didn't talk to me as I took the boat in through the entrance and anchored right at the head of the harbour, off the narrow beach of white shells. And then, almost grudgingly, she pulled out the binoculars and looked around.

"There's a cabin," she said, and twirled the focus knob. "Apple trees." The glasses swept round the shore and over the beach. "A couple of cherry trees and . . . " the knob turned again, " . . . berry bushes." She smiled. "I like this place."

We picked buckets of berries and, in the evening, Kristin got out the canning jars, set a big pot boiling on the stove.

Now the snow flurries round the window. "Remember how hot it was then?" says Kristin. I remember the sound her spoon made, screeching back and forth across the metal pot, then banging on the rim.

I sat on the V-berth as the noise shivered down my neck. Screech, screech, clang! Over and over. I glared at her over the top of the bulkhead, convinced she was doing it just to annoy me.

"Can't you use the spatula?" I said.

"Oh, I could," she said, and the spoon squealed, "if you don't mind bits of plastic in your jam."

I went outside and stretched out in the cockpit. I said I couldn't stand it anymore.

"Stand what?" said Kristin.

"The noise."

"Does it bother you?" she said. "I didn't know it bothered you."

I said it felt like a cat scratching at my spine.

"I'll tell you what," she said. "I'll only stir in one direction."

I found it only half as annoying.

The jars that Kristin filled that day are empty now. "This is the last of the Kynumpt jam," says Kristin, mopping at her plate with a bit of the egg-soaked toast. Outside, icy snow whispers on the roof.

But there are still some jars from Calvert Island down on the basement shelves. When winter turns to spring, it'll be good to go there again. We'll pull off the jar lid and smell sea air touched with sand and the huckleberry patch of Pruth Bay.

Kristin calls it her jam diary. I call it summer in a jar.

In the Dark

WHEN THE SUN SET, I WENT UP ON DECK. I closed the hatch to seal off the cabin lights, and I sat there watching the darkness close in around me.

It was the type of night I like best on a boat, when you can look over the side and see nothing at all, as though the world ends there at the edge of the deck and if you slip overboard, you'll just keep falling, tumbling, forever.

It was such a huge blackness that I clung to the mainsheet where it stretched down from the block, the way a child reaches for your hand before he peers over the gulf of a stairway's bottom step.

There was no moon, no stars, just a line of bony trees a little blacker than the sky, looming nearer as the night grew thick and dark. All around, the water was blackboard smooth, holding the dim shadows of land so still on its surface that they might have been etched in the water.

I heard a salmon jump, and then another, for we were off the mouth of a spawning stream. Up in the trees, branches crackled in the undergrowth, and the whole shoreline crept toward me.

I don't know why I got out the spotlight. Maybe to see what was out there; maybe to break up the darkness or hold it at bay. But I swept a circle of light along the shore, over stumps and dead trees that seemed to jump back from the beam like a forest of headless, armless men. Then I aimed it down at the water, into a grey mist of swirling dust.

Out of the gloom came an animal. It had the body of an eel and a big, bulbous head. It wriggled orange and yellow up through the cone of light, then down again, into darkness.

When I switched off the spotlight, the shoreline leapt forward by yards.

In the silence, from the north and far away, a rumble started. It was like faint thunder or the sound of distant rapids. And it grew louder, and louder still, until a big jet went booming past above the clouds.

I imagined the people up there, rushing forward in tidy rows, clutching onto seat backs as they peered down through all that blackness. They wouldn't even see the tiny glow of damp teak as they hurtled past overhead.

The world didn't seem so very big to me anymore nor so very wild. By the time I got the hatch open and the spotlight back in its bracket, the plane was a hundred miles away, but I could still hear the engines as I turned off the lights and went to bed.

"See anything out there?" said Kristin.

"Not much," I said. "A bulb-headed fish."

"Hmmm," she said, half asleep. "You should be careful where you shine that light. You don't always want to see what's out there."

"The land is rocky, glowing gold with seaweed."

The Truth About Scotchmen

THE SKIPPER WAS FROM THE PRAIRIES, A FARM BOY. He liked to fish beyond the horizon, out in the Gulf where the waves rolled like grasslands, and the spume drifted across them like tossed chaff. He played country and western songs on the tape deck as the boat rolled along, tapping his feet to John Denver. And at night he anchored on the "shallow spot" where the bottom was still three hundred feet down, or just drifted with the tide and the wind and found himself at dawn in a new place that was exactly the same, but miles away.

It was all new to me. Not just a world without land—so unbroken and huge that you almost could believe the earth is flat and the sky a speckled bowl atop it—but everything to do with fishing boats and gear. I had to learn that *pigs* were slabs of Styrofoam and that *hoochies* were plastic lures that the skipper liked to bounce on his palm like dancing hula girls. I had to learn to laugh when he did that, and to eat his pancakes at breakfast, thick as bicycle tires, but a lot more rubbery.

I had to learn how the sea could change in hours from a steaming mirage to a wildly-tossing thing that sent spray flying over the cabin top and brought the boat to a shuddering stop with trolling bells jangling.

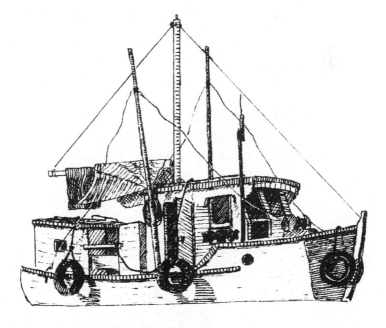

"Look," said the skipper, and tapped me on the shoulder. A wave was rolling up behind us, tall as the mast and streaked with foam. I ducked down in the cockpit and waited for it to crash over the deck. Then the boat rose with the wave, heaved and shuddered, and the skipper was looking down at me. He was laughing. "I've done that too," he said. "A hundred times."

He woke me once, long before dawn, to watch a container ship steaming across the shallow spot on its way to Juneau. It was steering straight toward us, its mastheads in a glaring line, navigation lights gleaming red and green on the wave tops. I could hear it coming—a hum and a rush of water—and feel its propeller through the deck, vibrating. In the dim glow of instrument lights, everything in the fishboat was shaking and swaying.

The skipper peered through the window. Above him, the Loran set flickered, green sine waves washing over his face.

"A boat was hit by one of those ships last year," he said. "They were sleeping, and the ship hit them right behind the mast."

"What happened?" I said.

"It cut them in two." He tapped the window. "Look, she's turning now."

The ship's masthead lights were separating. In a moment, the red port light blinked out and the hull stretched, streaming phosphorescent wake.

The ship slid by a half-mile astern, and in the blackness of its passing, the sky was choked with stars. There were millions of them it seemed, in swirls and spirals, and the anchor lights of the fishing fleet made their own constellation on the water.

"They stuffed the engine room with Scotchmen," said the skipper, stepping back, yawning. "And they kept half of the boat afloat."

"Scotchmen?" I said. I had an image of kilted men in tartan cloth squeezing themselves down around the engine.

"Yes. It was close," said the skipper. "Every boat around came over with bladders and floats."

So, it was then that I learned that ships don't always *pass* in the night and that Scotchmen are fat rubber bladders filled with air. And we sat up until dawn with Johnny Horton on the tape deck, watching a black sea, and a milky way of fishing boats.

Whale Songs

EVERY DAY WE WENT A LITTLE FARTHER TO THE SOUTH, and every night we anchored somewhere new, in a different bay surrounded, like the last, by trees and rock. We watched the sun go down, the stars appear—the Dipper above us, Cassiopeia off to one side—every night the same arrangement, only turned a bit, as though in a kaleidoscope. And by midnight or so, the new place would seem identical to the last, just a smudge of black shore and the field of stars above.

Each night, Kristin settled under the skylight in the forward berth and said, "Put on a tape."

And I'd poke the cassette into its slot, start it going. I don't listen to a lot of music. In the last ten years, I've bought only one album, Judy Collins' *Colors of the Day.* So we played the same music in the same place, over and over and over again.

Then we ran into the whales. They were Orcas, going the same way we were, plowing in formation along a dead-straight line, rising together, falling together, steaming forward as purposefully as a naval task force. They passed us on each side, surrounded us ahead and astern and, for a moment, we might have been one of them, all heading south on a wonderful, mysterious voyage.

"Wow," said Kristin. We could hear them breathe, see the little flaps on their blowholes open and close. Without slowing, they pulled ahead and kept on going.

I don't know how it happened, but we decided if we played music for them, the whales might stay around. So I went below and poked the cassette back in its slot. I turned up the volume and the music came blasting out, *Farewell to Tarwathie,* with its weird, haunting whale songs.

It thundered through the boat. It made the rigging vibrate like guitar strings; the cries of the whales screamed through inch-thick planks and blasted down into the sea twelve hundred feet deep. I twisted the knob until it wouldn't go any further.

I had to yell to Kristin over the music and the engine. "Is it working?"

She screamed back. "What?"

I said, "Is it working?" And the whales on the tape screeched and shrieked.

Kristin called through the hatch; I didn't have a clue what she said. I poked up my head, had a quick look around. I could almost see the music, shimmering like heat over the cockpit, the notes ricocheting in every direction. I said, "I can't hear you down there."

"What?" she said.

I yelled; I couldn't yell any louder than that. "I said I can't hear you."

"What?" She shook her head. "I can't hear a word you're saying."

"Oh, for God's sake," I said, and switched off the tape.

The Orcas were already half a mile away. Kristin said, "I think you scared them off."

We anchored that night in the same place again, right under the Dipper, just beside Cassiopeia. Kristin crawled into the berth, under the skylight. "Put on a tape," she said. "Anything but Judy Collins."

The Americans Come Ashore

THEY LOOKED LIKE MOVIE STARS, OR THEY THOUGHT THEY DID, I imagined.

It was hot when they came, with starfish wilting on the rocks, shrivelling into orange dwarf-stars in the sun. Their boats appeared from the heat-haze, shimmering for a while in the distance before they emerged as gleaming white motor yachts.

We saw the smoked-glass windows and the starched flags flown like battle ensigns from the transom. We heard the rattle of their anchor chain as they ran out. There were two boats, and each had a small floatplane lashed to an upper deck.

We watched them from the dock, where the boat beside us was slowly sinking, spewing out a river of oily bilgewater; where the tide was out and the mudflats, riddled like Omaha Beach with rusted bits of twisted metal, stank of sewage and old oil. Kristin sat with a handkerchief pressed to her face, masking the odor with a dab of perfume.

It was a working dock, filled with fishing boats and bashed-in tugs. All along it, people stopped what they were doing and looked up as one of the American couples came ashore. Mechanics in overalls and fishermen in Stanfield's shirts turned to watch them land.

She was dressed in white, with a bright scarf over her hair, and she had a

coifed poodle on the end of a braided leash. He was very tall, with a tanned face and clothes of peach and lemonade colors, in layers, so that he stood out in the sunshine and the heat like a chilled, cool Singapore Sling.

The breeze lifted the corner of her scarf as they strolled up the dock, the poodle snaking in front of them across the planks. Every time they passed someone, they stopped and stood inches away, and when they smiled it was like looking at the glittering keyboards of concert pianos.

When he spoke, his voice was like a finely-tuned Rolls Royce engine. It purred, and you could have balanced a three-penny bit across his tongue as he spoke. "Hi," he said, "how ya doin'?"

No one answered, though, not the mechanics with their hands full of box wrenches and their pockets stuffed with rags, nor the fishermen with their Stanfield's arms wrapped around boxes of gear and rolls of charts.

Only their heads turned as the Americans passed. Then the piano teeth were right in front of me and he was purring, "Hi. How ya doin'?" with his peach-colored shirt rippling in the wind. And it seemed, then, as though the heat had eased a bit and the mud stank a little less.

But I couldn't answer, either, and only muttered something as they passed, feeling as awkward as a child forced to greet his parents' friends.

They didn't stay long at the dock. They walked once to the end and back again. Then he took the poodle in his arms and held it as she stepped first into the tender.

They looked different as they motored off across the bay, as the heat and smells closed in again around the dock, as they grew smaller and smaller with the distance.

They looked lonely, in a way, or they thought they were, I imagined.

The Captain Who Went
Up With His Ship

THERE WAS A GALE WARNING THE DAY OF THE RACE; the captain took the helm of his Hobie Cat. I had a feeling that day, a premonition, I guess. As we sailed out to the starting line I asked my friend what to do if his catamaran should capsize.

He told me the mast would hit the water and the boat would stay like that, with the deck just beyond the vertical, one hull in the water and one in the air. Then we'd both stand on the lower hull, he said, and pull the little boat upright again. "Just go to the low side," he said.

The low side. Go to the low side. I nodded.

"You won't even get your feet wet," he promised.

We were racing against boats twice the length and more of the captain's Hobie. Already they were milling at the start, heeling far over as gusts of wind swept down from the shore. We could see the gusts, bands of black that rippled across the water.

"We'll come down on the line and gybe onto the starboard tack," the captain said. He put the helm over. A ratchet clicked as he wound in the mainsheet and the Hobie surged forward.

"Tacking," the captain said.

In calm weather, it's easy to turn a Hobie Cat. You sit on the trampoline that joins the hulls and, when the boom comes across, you duck your head, then shuffle to the other side of the boat. In a blow, you hurl yourself across; your weight on the weather side is all that keeps the boat upright.

I let the jib sheet fly; we squirmed under the boom as it scythed above us. I hauled in the sheet. Behind me, the ratchet was clicking again. The big boats were well up the harbour, a crowd of tilted sails racing for the weather mark. A streak of wind rushed toward us and sent the Hobie shooting forward with a whistle of rigging.

"Get ready to go out," the captain said.

I sorted out the trapeze wire that led to the masthead. I could dangle from it, like a spider, and lie flat above the water with my feet on the side of the hull. I clipped it to my harness and watched the wind come tearing down.

"Out, out!" said the captain. The Hobie heeled in the gust.

And I stepped over the side. It's exciting to ride like that, suspended almost parallel to the waves and four feet above them. Tilted up on one hull, the boat nearly flies, and you roar along in a cloud of spray.

Then the gust swept past, and the hull dropped.

"In, in," said the captain.

The big racers were closer now, the nearest only a few boat lengths away. Another gust came rippling over the water.

"Out, out," the captain said. For a moment, water lapped against my boots, feathering past my legs, and then the gust died down. "In, in," he said, and wiped his brow. "Oh, this is going to be exhausting."

We passed Cow Bay with water frothing between the Hobie's hulls. We gybed past the mark and the Hobie settled into an easy reach, boiling along with the boom pushed out. The next buoy whizzed past, and when we tacked again off the leeward mark, the wind was rising, and the bands of black were thick and close together.

"Out, out," the captain said.

The hull came up, steadied, and rose again, until I was almost standing on its edge. It rose further and the captain freed the mainsheet. Line whirred through the blocks; the sails flapped and the boat fell upright. It dropped me on the water like a tea bag on a string.

"In, in," he said.

One by one, the big boats slid quietly behind us. The captain was working up to the mark when the wind shifted a few degrees and the boat shuddered.

"Tacking," the captain said.

The next gust hit the sails all aback. The Hobie tilted slowly over and the masthead hit the water. "The low side," I thought, "the low side." And I stepped onto the only flat surface I could see, which happened to be the mast. With a gurgle and a splutter, the boat turned upside down.

It was as easy as walking down a flight of stairs. I stepped from the mast to the cross beam to the overturned hull. I stood there, astride a narrow ridge of fiberglass, as the captain came up from under the boat. He hauled himself through the mainsheet like Neptune rising from the depths. Water poured out of his jacket, gushed from his sleeves and dripped down his beard.

I was pretty pleased with myself. "You were right," I told him. "I didn't even get my feet wet."

I balanced on the hull, and my friend stood on the trampoline with the waves slopping over his boots. From the shore, it must have looked as though we were standing on water. One of the big boats had already hauled down its sails and was motoring back toward us when the real miracle happened.

It appeared from nowhere, shining and huge, throbbing with power. A tug boat. Suddenly it was there and, when it came alongside, I hopped up on the deck. But the captain, a stickler for tradition, insisted on staying with the boat.

The tug pulled; the Hobie came upright. And the captain, spread-eagled over the hull, went up with his ship.

Biscuits for Breakfast

I WAS FILLETING FISH when a sailboat came gliding into the bay, gleaming and huge. It was twice the size of our little *Nid*, a real boat, the type of ocean sailor I'd always dreamed of having. The mast was as tall as the trees, rigged with strands of pure silver. The sails were stowed in tailored bags that matched the highlights of the hull—a deep and regal blue.

I watched it with envy. *Nid* was cramped and slow, and though she was ours—and that was a bit of a consolation—she would never be big enough, or good enough, for what I wanted to do. This newcomer was the perfect boat, a ghost ship from my dreams come to haunt me with expectations unfulfilled.

I watched it with my hands held out, dripping slime and blood. The fish we'd caught that morning sprawled halfway across the cockpit.

"Oh, it's a beauty," said Kristin, in the hatch. I didn't know if she meant the salmon or the sailboat.

"*Sandra Light*," I said, reading the name across the bow. The boat was nearly twice the length of ours, and the closer it came the more *Nid* seemed to shrink. By the time it anchored close ahead, I felt like a Fisher-Price captain jammed in a little toy boat.

Kristin picked up the filleting knife. "You know," she said, "we can't eat all this ourselves."

"No?" I said.

She shook her head. "We'll have to give away at least a quarter of it."

I looked around. The bay was empty except for us and *Sandra Light*. "Who to?"

She pointed with the knife. There were shining scales speckled along the blade, as though she'd been slicing up rainbows.

"No," I said, and she smiled. She guessed what I was thinking.

"If we wait until a boat comes in that looks more impoverished than ourselves, we'll be here a long time."

But I knew who we'd find on a boat like *Sandra Light*. There would be a young man in a lemon-colored shirt, in yachting pants with a crease ironed in. He'd have sunglasses dangling on pink cords, canvas deck shoes with the little plastic tips still attached to the laces. It would be the guy from Port Hardy who, annoyed at my dog, had forced a grim smile and said, "Shall I kill her now, or later?" Yes, it would be him, or his clone.

It might be the guy who'd tried to jam his forty-foot boat into a tiny cove and then told me, with his hands on his hips, "You're taking up the whole bay with your little boat." I'd hated that. *My little boat.*

"So what do you want to do?" asked Kristin.

"Maybe a kayaker will come in," I said. "He'd appreciate it, a little guy like that."

Kristin picked up a fillet. "Anyone would appreciate this." It was two pounds of flesh as red as autumn apples. "Come on. We'll take it over right now."

The deck was almost too high to reach from the dinghy. Kristin called, "Hello," and nobody answered. She knocked timidly on the hull.

I knew what they were doing inside. They were sitting with tall glasses filled with crackling ice, hoping we'd go quietly away.

"Hello," she said again. And a head came out through the cockpit awning, then another one.

This wasn't right. They were thirty years older than they should have been. The man wore a plaid shirt faded from the sun; the woman wore a flowered blouse. When they smiled, their eyes smiled too. "Hello," they said.

Kristin held up the fish. "We have too much," she said. "Would you like a piece?"

They grinned. They reached down and took the fish, and started talking about where they were going and where they'd been, and how hard it was to work a big sailboat when you're getting old. Then they thanked us again, wished us a good voyage, and a good night.

In the morning, we heard a timid knock on *Nid*'s hull. They floated alongside, the two of them, in a dinghy so small they had to stretch their arms to reach the deck. The lady passed up a stainless-steel pan. "I made some biscuits," she said. "Would you like some?"

They were still warm, wrapped in a checkered towel, a dozen biscuits that lasted through the day, until we tied up at Bella Bella. I still had the rope in my hand when a fisherman came down the dock. He tipped back his head and smiled at little *Nid*. "Could I see inside?" he asked.

I warned him, "It's pretty small."

"Oh, that doesn't matter," he said. "Anything you can call your own today is good enough."

A Cold Crossing

THE COLDEST NIGHT OF THE YEAR. The last thing I wanted was to leave the warmth of the house and cross the harbour in an open boat. From the window I could *see* the cold out in the meadow, waiting for me.

A moon, one night past full, floated over the mountains like a bubble of gold. It covered the snow with sparkles and glitter, as though the stars had fallen there upon the meadow. In the sky, in the light of the moon, only Orion was left. He was a ghost in a silvery shroud.

But somewhere up there, at six hundred miles an hour, Kristin was hurtling home from a trip to the south. She would land at the airport just a few miles away, but we both had to cross the harbour to meet at the terminal in town. She would ride in a highway coach on the airport ferry. I would cross in the skiff, then drive from the dock to the terminal.

She was just leaving Vancouver when I filled a Thermos with coffee for the trip across. As I pulled on a pair of quilted pants, my snowboots, a coat padded with sheepskin, she passed over Gibsons and up the Sunshine Coast. I unearthed a long woolen scarf from the depths of a closet and stepped out through the door as she thundered over Powell River.

All around, the moonlight shone in the snow like animal eyes. And the dog, seeing them, squared off with a series of barks that shivered like bells through the frozen trees.

The tractor wouldn't start, and I struggled with it as Kristin raced up the coast, over Desolation Sound, over Quadra Island. I poured the first cup of coffee over the choke; my fingers froze to the handlebars.

Then the tractor started with a roar, and the headlight cast a huge shadow of the dog against a bank of snow. The dog barked. She bounced and yapped. And when she ran ahead of me, her shadow seemed to chase her right down the hill. It loomed up from the darkness and sprang out from snow-covered stumps. Now ahead and now behind. At every corner it was there again, bounding from the forest with a suddenness that shocked her. And I laughed at her as we shot down the path, while Kristin crossed Knight Inlet on her way north.

It was even colder at the dock, in a north wind honed by the water. Icicles clung to the fenders; the mooring lines were lengths of twisted pipe. I had to chip out the bilgewater in big, jagged chunks. The outboard wouldn't start. My toes went numb. Icy bird beaks pecked at my fingers and cheeks. Somewhere to the south, Kristin came whistling over a snowy wasteland.

I poured two cups of coffee on the fuel lines and gas cap. The steam swirled up and froze, coffee scented, on my scarf. It smelled wonderful, and warm.

In the harbour, the sea was smoking. Thin wisps of icefog swirled on the surface. We went puttering, sputtering toward town as Kristin circled right above us.

She was landing when I poured my last cup of coffee and breathed that steam again, when I felt the warmth through my fingers. She was slowing in a howl of downthrusters and swirling snow when I rocked the boat and accidentally spilled the last of my coffee in the bilge.

I scraped ice from the car windows with a dinghy oar, and beat her to the terminal by just a few minutes. She was wearing gloves and a scarf when she stepped from the bus.

"It's so cold," she said. "So cold."

"I know," I said. "I just . . . "

"Oh, it was freezing at the airport!"

"I know," I said. "I had to . . . "

"And they didn't have the heater on!"

"You poor thing," I said.

She thumped her hands together. "I can hardly wait to get in the boat and cross the harbour. It will be so good to be warm again."

"I have to stop for a coffee," I said.

"Do you have to?" she asked. "I'd really like to get home and get warm."

"It's not for me." I stooped down and picked up her bag. It was easy; my hand was frozen into a hook. "I was thinking of the outboard."

The Canvas
Deck Bucket

THERE COMES A POINT during every project when I throw up blood-stained hands and say, "Why am I doing this?"

With mechanical work, it's the moment the wrench slips off a rusted bolt for the third time and my knuckles jam up against the teeth of the cranking gears; the moment the wrench plunks down again in the icy bilge water below the engine. With woodwork, it's when the hammer hits my thumb once too often, or I work the jigsaw round in a circle right through its own cord.

"Why am I doing this?" I say. And having said it, I can fish out the wrench, or splice the wires back together, and finish the job. I call it perseverance. Kristin calls it self-mutilation.

"What are you working on now?" she asked, seeing the Band-Aids on my fingers.

"A canvas deck bucket," I told her, and showed her the drawing in the book of marlinespike seamanship; it was a beautiful piece of handiwork, a thing right out of the fo'c's'le of the *Cutty Sark*. It was all rope and wood and laid-up grommets, the perfect Christmas present for my father. That year, at the age of 71, he bought the first sailboat he'd had in half a century. He had always loved traditional things, like bowsprits and ratlines and ropes that are properly whipped.

"Your dad will like this," said Kristin. "It's a handsome thing." She didn't ask how someone can cut himself with a canvas bucket; she knew me well.

I sewed up the heavy cloth until my hands were as prickled as pincushions. I cut out the wooden bottom, turned it on edge, and sawed out a shallow groove. When the saw slipped off for the fifth time, and left another ragged line of triangles along my thumb, I threw it down on the bench. "Why do I do this?" I cried, then wrapped an old sock round my hand and finished sawing.

A day or two later, Kristin was watching me work. She looked down at my tools spread out on the table. "Why do you need a calculator to make a bucket?" she asked.

"I had to figure out the circumference," I said.

She looked like someone who'd just bitten into a lemon. "You mean sailors

129

didn't make canvas buckets before someone invented the calculator?"

"I don't have a clue how they made them," I said. And it was obvious by then that I didn't have a clue. My bucket was lopsided and twisted like an old boot. It didn't look much like the one in the picture: too thick and stiff to fold up, too riddled with needle holes to carry water from one end of the boat to the other. But still, it was a bucket, and all of the ropes were whipped at the ends.

"It's a nice bucket," said Kristin. "I hope your father won't get it too dirty."

"Or too wet," I said.

She laughed. "Maybe you should write on it: 'Keep Dry.'" She took it in her hands, tapped the bottom. "It is a nice bucket." She looked at the hem as crooked as a cat's tail, at the rope ring that ended up half an inch short even with a calculator. There was a tiny drop of blood on the canvas, at the end of a line of clumsy stitches.

"I hope he knows I made it."

"Oh," she replied, "I don't think there'll be any doubt."

Putting Down
The Ritz

IT WAS THE SUN FILTERING THROUGH THE TREES that showed us where the thing sat, so hidden in a grove of cedars that we'd already walked past it once before. Long shafts of sunlight stabbed at the branches and the evening fog, like swords of the Jedi knight, thrusting through the forest. The shafts hit the top of the *thing,* and came glaring back to us as we lay at anchor in a bay without a name.

"It's a longhouse," I said. I imagined cedar shakes aged to brittle whiteness, and thought we'd found something unseen for two hundred years.

"A sheet of plastic," said Kristin, who saw just another bit of squalor in the wilderness. She grumbled: "I'm tired of seeing ruined things."

But she climbed in the dinghy with me, and we rowed to a shelf of rock where someone had made a mooring from an iron ringbolt; rusty and scaly now, the ring was no thicker than a lady's bracelet. There was still a trail worn into the lichens and the moss, and we walked up toward the *thing* in the forest.

"We were both wrong," said Kristin.

The thing was a house—a huge, towering house with vast windows looking out on the forest. Up by the eaves, where the sunlight glinted off a roof of corrugated tin, a circle of leaded glass was set in the wall, tiny panes of all colors spelled out "The Ritz."

Kristin stepped up on the porch and knocked on the door. She called out in a voice that didn't carry far through the forest, then moved to the window and peered inside. But The Ritz was empty.

"I don't think there's been anyone here for years," said Kristin the next morning, after a walk in the woods. "There's a 1987 catalogue hanging in the outhouse. And a few pictures taped to the walls inside the house."

"You went inside?" I said.

She shrugged. "The door wasn't locked." She said there was a tourist pamphlet from Saskatchewan laid out on the counter. "I think someone from the prairies had a summer cottage here. And he just hasn't made it back for a while."

If that was so, he'd picked a place as unlike Saskatchewan as anything he could find. The Ritz was in a muskeg clearing surrounded by mournful trees; in a valley surrounded by rocky hills; on an island surrounded by water.

"Inside, everything's dry and dusty," said Kristin. And that made sense. He would have tried to keep it that way, the flatlander. To remind him of home.

So I went and had a look inside The Ritz myself. There was a little fridge and a sink full of spiders, some bedding left on a high shelf. And there was that big tin roof that must have rattled in the rain like snaredrums.

I didn't think the man who built The Ritz had come from Saskatchewan. This place was too foreign for that. He *liked* it closed in, gloomy and wet. He must have come from the coast.

He'd lived in Kitimat maybe, 75 miles to the east; or even Rupert, the same distance to the north. And he'd come here for the summers and the salmon. But soon he'd grown tired of the brooding trees, and the constant changing of the tide. And of those mountains looming all around, closing in.

I could see him sitting on his plywood bench, there by the fuel-barrel stove, dreaming over his little book about Saskatchewan. And one day he had just packed it all in, and moved to a place where he could see a hundred miles in every direction.

Why right this minute he was maybe sitting on the porch of a farmhouse, telling someone about his old home on the coast and how dreary it was. He had his feet up on the railing, brown dust falling from his boot soles. And he was happy now, putting down The Ritz.

The Lost Moose
of Lucy Island

THE FIRST REPORTS WERE OF FOOTPRINTS. Huge ones. A crackling in the bush and a feeling that something was out there, watching.

It was big, whatever it was. Noises like a man would make, said the people who heard them. Tracks as big as pie plates, said those who saw them crisscrossing lonely beaches.

Kristin came running in. "There's a moose loose!" she cried. "There's a moose loose on Lucy!"

"Impossible," I said. And laughed sarcastically.

Well, it didn't make sense. A moose wandering a coastal island? A moose a hundred miles or more from its little moose house beyond the mountains? A moose, like Bullwinkle, with only squirrels for company?

"I believe it," said Kristin, who'd never seen a moose. Two months later we would spot one by the highway near Houston, would watch the moose step, lazily, over a five-foot wire fence. "THAT's what's loose on little Lucy?" she would say of this monstrous horse in a cheap fur coat. "Oh, the poor thing. The poor thing."

But now, she crossed her arms and said again, "Well, I believe it."

"A moose?" I said. "How would it get there?"

"Down the river," she said, "caught in a current." She said it so simply that I almost believed it was possible. After all, we'd seen deer a long way from shore, paddling along as happily as dogs chasing sticks. I could imagine a moose clinging to uprooted trees, turning round and round as the river bore him down over sandbars and shoals, striking off for distant land when cold, saltwater waves knocked him from his raft.

So winter passed and spring arrived. And the expeditions started. People went off in search of the moose—or whatever it was—with children as camera bearers. And scattered reports came back: more tracks; more crackling in the bush; and dark shapes, moving.

In February, we mounted our own expedition and sailed to Lucy Island in search of the creature. But it was too stormy to land—breakers burst on the shore, can buoys rocked like carnival horses, a wave slopped over the stern. So we turned back for home with no sign of the moose.

Then it happened. Someone saw the moose. It hurtled past her, a poor frightened thing, huge and hulking, crashing from bush to beach. And I was convinced.

"They should save it," I told a friend on the dock. "They could airlift it out, fly it up the river."

"All that for a moose?" she said. "Moose aren't exactly endangered."

I said, "That one is." It seemed everyone had heard of the moose by then. It was a walking freezer-pack of roast and ribs and steaks.

"But it's still a moose," she said. "Maybe if it was a Kermode bear, they'd do something."

Well, there was an idea, I thought. I could phone up and say, "There's a Kermode loose on Lucy Island!"

And they'd say, "Impossible," and laugh sarcastically.

In the Pinks

L ATE IN THE SEASON, we came upon
a salmon stream. We anchored off
its mouth, on the far side of a ledge
that was dry and bare on the evening
tide. All around the boat, the fish leapt
and jumped, like sandfleas on a beach,
popping their heads above the surface as
night settled on that lonely bay.

By morning, the fish were quiet. The tide
was rising; it covered the ledge and swirled at
the mouth of the creek, holding back the stream
in shallow, rocky pools. Before we set off for shore, I dropped a dipnet in the
dinghy.

"What's that for?" Kristin asked, when it landed at her feet. I didn't answer;
I was busy digging out the filleting knife.

She kicked the net down under the thwart, jammed its telescoping handle
below the rubber seat. "You're not going to catch one, are you?"

"I just want to look," I said, and climbed down beside her.

We landed at the creek, swollen by a week of rain. Water chuckled through
a jumble of smooth, algae-covered stones, tumbled over natural dams from
pool to pool, and in the lowest one, the fish were waiting.

They'd lined up nose to tail, skidding left and right as their bodies wiggled
in place, struggling against the current. In the dark creek water, they shim-
mered blue and emerald green, the colors of the stones and algae. But when
they rose, broke the surface with dorsal fin and hunchback, they seemed grey-
er, older. Within a week, every one of them would be lying dead on the creek
bank. It seemed an awful waste, all those steaks and fillets floating there.

Kristin left and went splashing upstream. I dug out the dipnet and snapped
it open. I looked for a fat salmon and lowered the net toward the water. The
handle tapped the rocks with a sound like a tolling bell.

The salmon milled about the pool in a sluggish, drunken crowd, like the
old grey men who open bars in the morning. It would be so easy to scoop one
up, I thought. I sank the net among the stones, and slid it in front of a big, fat
salmon. Others crowded round; brushing against the metal bar. It would be so
easy, I could do it with my bare hands.

Two years before, those fish had gone reeling and spinning through the pool, inch-long babies swept along by the spring runoff, spilled out by the thousands into salt water. They'd gone a thousand miles or more out to sea, a thousand miles back again. They'd avoided nets and troll lines, seals and whales, returning to the very same spot they'd started from. It seemed impossible; almost magic. I wondered how they found it again, this little stream in the middle of nowhere. I wondered, too, if the place seemed smaller than they remembered.

It would have been so easy to catch one. But I couldn't do it. And when Kristin came back downstream, her boots skidding on the bottom of the creek, knocking aside stones with chunky thuds, she found me sitting on a round boulder with the net propped beside me.

She said, "You're not trying to catch them, are you?"

"Of course not," I said.

"Good." She stood at the edge of the pool, watching the fish pushing against the stream. "Because it wouldn't be fair. Not when they've come this close."

"We'll catch one tomorrow," I said, "out in the Sound." And she nodded. "Anyway, they'll be bigger tomorrow."

The Lady Vanishes

I FOUND THE BOAT HALF UNTIED, scraping against the pilings as she swung in the wind. The bow line was loose. It snaked across the dock and dipped its tail in the water. Across the thwarts lay her jacket, its sleeve reaching up over the gunwale. The dock was empty.

Two hours earlier, Kristin had left for town. "I'm taking my boat," she said. "I'll be home in the evening."

I could see her Thermos in the boat now, a puddle of tea that had leaked out around the stopper. Her little Pelican flashlight, guaranteed to survive everything except bear attacks and two-year-olds, poked out from a jacket pocket. So she'd come this far, before she vanished.

A boat's wake slopped up against the dock. It rocked the boat, and the bow swung round, crunching at the crust of barnacles on the pilings. Kristin's Thermos bottle rolled along the thwart, dripping cold tea.

The water lapped against the pilings, painting dark priests' collars above the surface. It set the float rocking, and the ramp rolled in its track, clanking and squealing on a rusted drum. Underneath, the water surged and smacked on weed-covered timbers.

Suddenly, the dog put her head down and sniffed between the planks.

There's a space under the dock, a black and oily place between the water and the planks. The dog once disappeared from the dock, and we found her trapped there, perched on a slippery timber and shivering from the cold. We had to get a crowbar, and pry up the dock timbers to get her out again.

She sniffed, and whined now.

I imagined Kristin coming down in her sandals and town clothes. She'd have tossed her jacket in the bow, thumped the Thermos down on the seat. She'd have untied the bow line and stepped on the gunwale. And the boat would have slid out from underneath her.

"Kristin!" I called. But it was two hours since she had left.

I knelt beside the dog and peered with her through the cracks in the planks. An old log rolled against the framework, a bit of bark twisted in the tide.

It's funny what you think about sometimes. I remembered Christmas

Eve when I was young, and hearing the news on the radio that there'd been a terrible car wreck at a nearby ski resort. I remembered my mother smoking cigarettes one after the other, nearly crying, not wanting to tell us Dad had gone there to buy us skiing lessons for a present. Then I thought of Kristin's mother, who's so hard of hearing, and how I'd have to shout through a thousand miles of phone lines to tell her that her daughter had drowned.

"Hmmm?" she'd say. "Found what?"

But of course Kristin must have gotten a ride. I imagined her coming down the ramp in her sandals, throwing her floater coat in the boat, thumping down her Thermos. She'd have untied the bow line. Then a little speedboat would have bumped up against the dock, surprising her, and she'd have left everything there to climb in beside her friend for the trip to town.

So I went home, and phoned her office. "No," they said. "We haven't seen Kristin all day."

She came home later in the afternoon, laughing, a sprig of wildflowers in her hand. She'd been at school in the morning; I'd forgotten that.

"Did I leave my boat untied?" she said.

"Yes," I said, and told her how I'd found it.

"The water taxi came," she said. "I was just ready to leave, and the water taxi came. I guess I should have phoned you."

"You might have," I said.

"But I forgot. And then I thought you'd figure it out anyway. You weren't worried, were you?"

"Worried?" I said. "No, not much." And I crushed out my cigarette in a heap of butts.

A Boat in the Hand

Ⅰ N THE FAIR-WEATHER DAYS BETWEEN the first storm of the year and the last frost of the winter, I decided to build a boat. I sat on the front steps with a handful of cat food, flinging the pellets one by one into the flower garden. And while the dog sniffed around, tracking down each tiny bit of food between the stumps of last year's plants, I built the boat for the first time in my mind.

It was a pretty thing, with a graceful sheer and just a bit of rocker to the hull. I fitted it with oars and the lateen sail I'd packed around for twenty years. I could already smell the fresh paint and the linseed oil, sticky in the sunshine.

The dog barked. I threw another piece of cat food down among the winter weeds and I launched the little boat, heading out across the harbour. It heeled, and steadied there with water boiling at the bow. I skimmed along with the sheet in one hand, the tiller in the other, and the boat made no wake at all, I'd designed it so well. I had sailed all the way to Cow Bay before the dog barked again and I had to stop to toss a bit of food.

I built the boat for the second time in the days that followed. A little at a time I worked, taking moments when Kristin wasn't home. She knew my legacy of boat-building, and how the Lawrences are as renowned for that as the Dionnes were for planned parenthood.

In the evenings I cut and taped, and only two days later I'd finished that second boat. The planks didn't fit quite right at the transom, and there was a bit of a gap between the bottom and one side. Bits of tape stuck up here and hung down there, but it was a nice little thing. I sat the model on my hand and went sailing across the harbour again.

I sat up on the gunwale in a freshening wind, and the boat went sliding down the waves. Flecks of spray spattered on the sail, but not a drop came over the side. I could smell the salt, hear the flutter of the sail and the hum of the sheet when it stretched taut. And at night, when the sun set, I rowed it home down a sliver of moonlight, the oars creaking in their thole pins.

"What are you going to do with that?" asked Kristin. She touched the model and set it rocking on my palm.

"Row it," I said.

"Row it?" She laughed. "You hate rowing."

Well, yes, that was true. The only thing I ever do with the oars in Kristin's boat is sit on them. Oh, once in a while I might take one off the thwarts and use it to pry the boat off the beach. I did row home one night when the motor broke down, but it's hard to row in half a gale, especially when there's nowhere to sit.

"I think it's a good boat for rowing," I said, and made the model scoot across my hand.

"It's a lovely boat," she said. "When are you going to build it?"

But I was off again, the boat sliding through the water. There's no hurry to build the third version. I'm too busy sailing it just like it is.

Picking Up Janet

IN AN ABANDONED HOUSE, AMID PILES OF FORGOTTEN THINGS, I saw a woman's face staring up from the floor. Her mouth was open in an awful scream, her eyes wide with horror. So it was no wonder I didn't recognize her immediately as Janet Leigh.

I stooped down to clear the rubble around her, and uncovered an old copy of *Psycho*. The book was thin and dusty, brown pages speckled with mildew.

Above the picture of Janet Leigh was stamped in big, red letters. "Warning!" it said. "This book is not to be read at night. Especially if you are alone . . . *Especially not at night!*"

I took the book with me as we wandered through the remains of the old settlement. There wasn't much left, just gaps in the undergrowth, and a few sagging rooftops. Here and there stood rusted stovepipes, twisted and bent, and bits of machines lay scattered around.

Behind the homesteads, the ground was flat and swampy. We found a trail past bogs and dry lake beds, the lines of footprints—adults and a child—hardened in the mud. We found old wolf tracks there, and bits of silver hair stuck to burred branches.

That night, long before the moon rose ghostly in a sky of black, we turned on the cabin lights and started *Psycho*. We read it aloud, taking turns, as breaths of wind sighed through the abandoned houses, as water lapped against the boat. We read for hours, until we were halfway through the book and the wolves started howling from the bog.

It was an eerie, moaning sound at first, so distant and faint. Then others called, closer, and the voices wailed through the woods around us. And Norman Bates crept from the pages of *Psycho*.

We heard his footsteps in the sounds of the boat, his breathing in the wind. We *felt* him out there, in the terrible calls of the wolves.

In the morning, the place seemed different. The abandoned house, its weathered boards warped from sun and rain, seemed a lot like the Bates motel. The bogs were deeper, blacker than they'd been the day before, and the rusted old stovepipes reached up from the trees like groping arms.

Again, we set out along the trail of footprints. Soon we found fresh wolf tracks crossing the trail, and followed them along a sodden stream bed. Kristin looked at the tracks for a while, studying them. She laid a palm in one of the paw marks left among the human footsteps, and it was bigger than her hand.

We walked slowly along, past oozing bogs, past freakish trees dwarfed into sinister shapes. We thought of *Psycho,* and Norman Bates. And we hurried back in the late afternoon, watching the sun, waiting for the night.

It was barely dark when we opened *Psycho* again, and read through to the end. Again Norman Bates skulked around us. But there were no wolves that night, and no wind in the trees. And when we finished, Kristin said, "Well, that wasn't so scary."

We made one more trip to shore before we left that place. We put *Psycho* back in the house, standing it at the end of a row of other books on a twisted shelf. And at noon, we pulled the anchors free from the mud, and motored out of the bay.

Kristin leaned against the boom and watched the shoreline pass. "I like it here," she said. "We'll have to come back."

"Yes," I said, and added it to the list.

It is a long list, all the places that we've come to like for one reason or another. I'll remember the old settlement as the Bates place. The place where I picked up Janet Leigh.

One Man's Best Friend

My brother steers the boat while I go forward to lower one of the headsails, I wrote in my notebook one day out of Prince Rupert.

The wind's strong now. The boat's galloping over waves that hiss and boil around us. The sail cracks and whips in the wind as I lash it down.

When I looked up from the lined pages, my brother was watching me. His face was ruddy and brown from a day of sun and wind, and I wanted to thank him, again, for coming along to take the boat south for the summer.

"What are you writing?" he asked.

"Oh, nothing," I said, smoothing the book flat on the table.

We've got Skipper the dog in her safety harness and she's sitting beside him at the tiller, clipped to a wooden cleat, I wrote. *Man's best friend, they say, but they're both watching me with solemn faces. They look worried as I balance on the foredeck.*

Two days out of Prince Rupert, the wind backed to the southeast. We anchored in Captain Cove and took the Skipper to the beach.

"What are your columns going to be about?" Donald asked, kicking nonchalantly at a rock.

I shrugged. "I don't know."

"Do you have a general theme in mind?"

"Not really," I said. "But you'll probably be in them, if that's what you mean."

He fell silent for a while. " Then I'd better not fall overboard," he said.

We haven't spent as much time together in years, I wrote that night, *maybe not since our frigid little camping trip in the snow at Forbidden Plateau.* The Plateau was cold then, and at dawn birds kept landing on the roof of the tent. Donald was snoring in his sleeping bag while I lay staring up at the tent ceiling, hearing the tiny birds' feet and imagining grizzly-bear claws scratching at the canvas.

I wonder often what he's thinking, and if he's as happy as I am.

On the fourth night out, we anchored between two islands when the wind changed again to the south. Donald watched me warily when I picked up the notebook.

I was worried my brother might have changed. There are whole parts of his life I know nothing about. He's an art teacher now, instructing college students and giving shows in Vancouver and Toronto. I was afraid he'd outgrown me.

"What are you writing there?" he said, eyes narrow.

"Nothing," I said.

He talked about his trip to Europe the night he arrived, as we ate scallops for dinner with Kristin's parents. And he filled his plate from a salad bowl, finished that, and filled it again.

"You should try this," he said, and passed me the bowl. It was half filled with peaches and strawberries and sliced bananas.

I nudged him in the ribs, and whispered. "I think this is dessert."

"Oh," he said, and jostled my elbow furtively until I knocked over my wine glass and sent a rivulet of white wine across the table and into the prim, skirted lap of Kristin's mother.

"Sorry," I said, but we snickered and giggled between ourselves like little kids, me and the art teacher.

"I think we might be dragging anchor." Donald was standing in the hatchway, raindrops on his cheeks. Outside, the wind had hauled around to the north and waves were breaking on the rocks behind us.

Donald paddled off into the night in the dinghy and hauled up the stern anchor. He brought it back, then kept the boat going slowly ahead as I raised the main anchor and we set it again in the lee of the island.

When I snugged the line down on the bitt and turned back to the cockpit, there were two faces watching me as there had been that first morning, solemn and concerned. Donald had one hand on the Skipper, the other on the tiller.

My best friend—and my dog.

The Boat-Building Lawrences

I BUILT MY FIRST BOAT WHEN I WAS SEVEN YEARS OLD. I remember the year exactly, because it was the same summer that I planned to fly.

I'd spent hours with a pencil and a piece of paper, studying the warped sheets of linoleum that lay beside the garage. They'd been there so long that the grass below them was sickly yellow, laced by white worms and maggots.

Halfway through the summer vacation, I'd told my brother how I planned to cut lengths from the curved sheets and lash them to my arms. I explained how I'd leap off the garage roof and flutter about the backyard.

He laughed at that, of course, and derided the concept until I finally gave it up. There was no history of flying in my family; we were the boat-building Lawrences.

When I was growing up, there were always books of boat plans in the house, drawings of the little sloop my father talked of building. The books filled entire shelves, but that boat was never launched.

One year, Dad came home with a mould for a fiberglass cruiser. We bought yards of matting and gallons of resin from a grimy little man who smirked at us and said, "Be sure to wash your hands after you finish, before you touch your privates, you know." We laid one layer of cloth into it, and then the mould sat in the basement for two years, converted into a giant laundry hamper.

My brother, too, took to boat-building and after high school went into partnership to buy an old sailboat on Lake Huron. He spent every weekend in

the boatyard, gluing down the bowsprit, scraping out the rot and putting new screws on the rudder pintles. When he discovered the keel bolts were falling out, he sold the boat and went hitch-hiking across Canada.

So there's a little bit of a boat-building tradition in my background.

That first boat of mine was a trim little ocean liner. I could see her in my mind, gleaming white, and I planned to launch her in the river and send her downstream. I wondered how long she would take to reach the ocean, and which ocean she would reach. I set to work with a length of two-by-four and some scraps of wood from my father's workbench. I imagined that old wall stud making great voyages.

The cabins split when I hammered them on, though, and the decks were soon studded with the twisted heads of bent and broken nails. I sawed away at the plank to make a fine V-bow, sawing and sawing for hours until I had two shallow lines scored into the checkered wood. I gave up, then, and asked my father to finish the sawing. But that boat was never launched either, and I think she ended her days as a doorstop by the cellar steps.

My second boat came a couple of years later. She was smaller, with tooth-pick masts and red sails cut from frazzled tissue paper. I crammed her through the wide mouth of a ketchup bottle and set her a'sail on a lumpy sea of plasticene.

"What's that?" my brother said.

"It's Dad's birthday present," I told him, holding it up. "What are you going to give him?"

"Nothing," he said. "At least I'm not giving him a piece of junk like that."

It *was* a piece of junk, I guess, but my father praised it highly, and set it on the mantel shelf beside his most prized possessions. It was, after all, the only boat the Lawrences had ever launched.

Beach of Dreams

K RISTIN AND I WENT SOUTH BY BOAT; my parents came north with my brother by car. We met at Port Hardy, at the fishermen's dock, where the boats were packed as tight as dominoes.

Donald's Landcruiser was down to its lines under a load of kayaks and paddles, camping stoves and sleeping bags, pots and pans and tents, cameras and water jugs.

I said, "Do we have to take all this?" And Donald said, "Oh, no."

He picked out a tiny little bag and said, "I guess this can stay behind."

We wedged stuff in the cabin, we heaped stuff on the deck. We filled the kayaks and towed them behind us. And we anchored in late afternoon off a beach of sand and gravel at the bottom of an island.

It was a magical trip, going back in time to our summer vacations in a huge orange tent: by the seaside; in the forest; on the prairie. Big as a cabin, the tent had smelled of canvas and oil; with the lantern inside, it had glowed like campfire coals.

Donald's pup tent snapped open like an umbrella. We used boulders to weigh down the corners. I said, "I'll bet Dad keeps stubbing his toes on the boulders."

We were nervous about bears, and slept with little foghorns at our sides. Donald hauled the food so high in a tree that even giraffes couldn't reach it. Then he slept below it, wrapped like a sausage in his bivouac bag. In the middle of the night, when I woke to hear huge feet scrunching through the gravel, I almost gave my poor father a stunning blast with the horn.

We found an old baseball lying sodden among the driftwood logs, a stick to

use for a bat. We played by crazy rules that put the outfielders into kayaks and moved imaginary runners around the bases.

As the tide rose, our diamond narrowed to an isthmus, to a slender aisle, and we moved our markers and made a cricket pitch. And Dad played long-stop again, the first time since his boyhood in London.

Wearing Kristin's orange sunhat, he guarded a single wicket, a twisted stick capped by a clamshell. He batted and bowled, and ran like a boy, laughing when he knocked one for six. And Mom—tiny as a fairy—fielded the balls and worried about him.

If the trip was magical for us, it was more so for him. It made him young again.

That night he had a dream. "It was a wonderful dream," he said. He was back in his youth, on an English field, doing what he'd loved to do.

"I was playing cricket," he said. "I was batting, and the bowler kept complaining that there was only one wicket. He was furious. And I looked down, and I saw that the pitch was made of sand."

He sighed. "Oh, it was such a wonderful dream."

Trip of a Lifetime

KRISTIN WAS LAUGHING. "Guess where Queen Elizabeth is going to go?" she said.

"Where?" I said.

She said, "Guess."

I hate this game. I flapped my arms. "The Belmont?"

She scowled. "Just think of the most out-of-the-way place. The most outrageous place. The one place where you'd never expect to see the Queen of England."

I said, "But not the Belmont?"

"The Khutzeymateen!" she cried. And with a flourish, she dropped the Daily News on the coffee table.

I saw the headline and snatched it up. "Circumnavigating the Pole," it said, and there was a picture of them—young Vikings on an old boat—off to Europe across the top of Russia. I'd talked of that idea for years.

"Wow," I said.

"Don't look at *that* article," said Kristin. "Oh, I knew you'd see that first." She touched the page, and the paper wrinkled. Under her finger, the headline said, "Queen to Visit Grizzly Reserve."

"See?" Her hands went to her hips. "Can you imagine that? The Queen walking along those bear trails in her little shoes? Her little white gloves, her little hat?"

A tiny figure she'd be among those enormous trees, somberly dark in her London Fog raincoat, maybe one of those transparent cowls tied under her chin. She'd have her handbag hooked over one arm, a can of bear spray in her hand.

"It sounds sort of neat," I said, and my eyes strayed back to the next column. The Vikings would be in the Arctic before the Queen even arrived in Canada.

"She's flying in," said Kristin. "All those people that go with her everywhere, all those helicopters; they'll scare every bear out of the valley."

"I guess so," I said absently. Would it be cold in the Arctic even in August? There was only a six-week window for the whole trip from the Bering Sea to Norway.

"Why can't she go by boat?" said Kristin. "She could take one of the charter boats. She'd have more fun."

I turned the page. There was the *Daegmar Aaen* against the glaciers of Iceland. I knew that boat. I'd seen the Vikings leaving the harbour, wondered who it was with a topsail yard. I'd missed them by five minutes.

"*You* could take her," said Kristin. "Wouldn't that be fun, going up to the Khutzeymateen with the Queen? In the *Nid*?"

"I don't know," I said. The dog would want to sit in her lap. Skipper would smell the Corgies. And the Queen would pet the dog's head with her white gloves and try to nudge her down in the footwell. Frankly, I'd rather be in Siberia.

And we both sighed, dreaming our respective dreams . . . about the trip of a lifetime.

Trading Places

HE WORE A WHITE SHIRT WITH THE SLEEVES ROLLED UP, tucked into pants that were dark and shiny like his eyes. He sat on the dock, and patted the dog, and offered to trade boats.

"My boat's worth sixty thousand dollars," he said, though he wasn't bragging about it. "Most of that's the license plate. I have to renew it every year, just like a car. It costs me $700 a year."

He'd been a fisherman for almost fifty years. His wooden gillnetter was tied farther up the dock, painted white and blue, like a child's toy.

"She's got a good engine," he said. "Goes eight knots. Easy on fuel."

He admired our little sailboat, and said how lucky we were to travel in her all the time. "Even if it's only for the summer," he said. And he asked again if I wanted to trade boats.

"I'll give you two hours to decide," he said. "Then we can put all of your stuff on my boat, and I'll put all my stuff on yours, and I'll just go away for the rest of my life."

He was sixty years old, he told us, and he fished by himself. He'd work right to the end of the season, hauling his net for the last time at the close of the final opening.

"It gets me home for Christmas," he said. "But you can't make much money at it. Just enough."

He said he didn't like to hear fishermen complaining all the time. They spend too much time in the bars, he said. He'd never had a cigarette, never had a drink.

He leaned back with his hands spread across the dock rail.

"So what do you say?" he said. "You want to trade boats?"

He had a son who didn't want to fish with him. And a wife, he said, whom he never saw in the summer.

"But I'd like to just sail away. Keep going somewhere, forever."

He asked a lot of questions about *Nid:* how fast she'd go, where we'd gone in her. Sometimes, while he talked, he reached out and touched my shoulder. And when someone walked past on the dock, he said, "I'm trying to trade boats here. I want to spend all my time travelling."

He left school after grade four. He fished through World War II, when a big naval base had stood where the dock was.

"Right here," he said. "Right where you are now."

Then he stood up, putting his hands on his hips to straighten his back. He looked at the boat again, his eyes going up the mast, and down the length of the hull.

"I'll come back in two hours," he said, "and then we can trade."

Another fisherman passed along the dock, and he went off with him, his arm around the man's shoulder. Soon after, the little gillnetter steamed past, and his arm came out through the window, and waved.

I watched him go, like a salmon himself, travelling every year to the same waters. I thought, he's already found his dream.

Fog at the Edge

I USED TO LIVE IN TOWN, in a house overlooking the harbour, and I'd stare across at either trees or blackness, depending on the time of day. I'd think how nice it was to live there, on the edge of a wilderness like that.

Now I look out on a city by day, and at lights by night and think how nice it is to live just on the other side of that edge.

But in early fall and late spring, when the nights are clear and warm, mornings bring fog to Prince Rupert harbour. And the view is the same from both sides then.

In the city, they drive to work with their headlights on. They like the way the fog swirls along city streets and they like the way the air feels—wet and heavy and smelling of the sea. They like to hear the foghorns of unseen ships, deep moans that stir the soul.

On the far shore, others hear the horns and wonder if the ships are anchored or moving. They untie their little boats and motor out slowly into the gloom.

It's scary, travelling in fog. The land disappears behind you and in every direction there's nothing but a small patch of water walled by a circle of grey. The circle moves with you, and you're burrowing a tunnel through the fog.

Then you're a kid again, going down that long flight of stairs to the dark basement where the spiders live. And there's something moving in the shadows at the bottom.

The fog presses against you. It confuses your hearing, throws off your sense of direction, and distorts your vision. You see shapes looming through the mist; large objects look small and small ones look huge. You see two butterflies cavorting above the bow, then you look again and they've become a pair of seagulls soaring at the edge of your vision. You see a huge log ahead, but when you swerve to avoid it, it's only a stick.

For a moment, you're in the narrow, gas-lit lanes of old London listening to the footsteps of Jack the Ripper ringing on the cobblestones.

You steer one way and then the other, trying to keep the compass needle steady on a bearing you know by heart. After a while you swear the compass is wrong, that you're really turning in slow circles. When the ship's horn blasts you off your seat, you have no idea at all where it's coming from.

Now you're lost on the English heath, listening to the Baskerville Hound braying in the fog.

You look at your watch, again and again. You know you should have seen the lights from shore by now. You tell yourself you're off course, that you're heading out toward Ridley Island. You nudge the boat a little to the north, though the compass says go east, go east. You wonder if you've allowed for the rising tide. Maybe you've already been carried beyond Fairview Bay and you're running up the harbour. You nudge the boat a little to the south but the compass says go east.

Dim shapes appear and disappear. Shadows flicker and move. The water ripples past the boat, flat and lifeless. You hear a steady rumbling sound through the fog, and see lights ahead and you wonder: are they the lights of shore? Or the lights of a ship bearing down on you, its bow slicing like a knife through the water?

Suddenly you're in the mist-filled shower stall of the Bates Motel and you're Janet Leigh waiting for the curtain to slide open.

Out of the fog looms the *Queen of the North*, straight ahead, huge and white, her engines rumbling. But she's moored in her slip, and the Fairview docks are just to your right, materializing in the mist.

You hurry then, for the fog has made you late, and you arrive in a world of traffic and noise. You've crossed the edge from one world to another, and will happily stay there until the fog lifts again.

Harrowsmith **by Lamplight**

WE FOUND THE BOAT SHED IN A SHELTERED BAY BEHIND A SPIT OF LAND. It rose from the beach in a grove of cedars, massive beams nailed to the trees with long, bent-headed spikes. It had a peaked roof and open walls, all lashed together with scraps of gillnet that drooped from every corner like webs of giant spiders.

A crude steambox hung from the rafters, and the ground below was strewn with bits of plank ends, arcs of ribs, and a section of eight-sided timber cut from a mast. Along one wall hung a horse's feedbag and homemade tools, parts of a Coleman stove. and coils of fraying rope. Crazily-twisted nails lay rusting in a pink plastic tray, and a clutch of old leg-hold traps lay tangled on a stump.

"Maybe he built his boat and sailed away," Kristin said.

"Maybe," I said, poking through the rubble. "But he left his *Harrowsmiths* behind."

There was a pile of them, sodden and welded together by the rain. Every second month, I thought, he'd make the trip to Bella Bella—it would take him most of a day—and bring back the latest copy. I could imagine him reading the magazines at night beside his fire, rolling them up to swat at the black flies that still haunted the old shed. And maybe he'd measure the progress of his boat against the mounting pile of *Harrowsmiths*.

It was a gloomy place, with the light of a channel marker flashing into the cove every few seconds, illuminating the shed with a glow of ghostly blue in the mist. Maybe he'd even read his *Harrowsmiths* like that, a word or two at a time, marking his spot with a fingertip between the flashes of light.

There was something sad in that wad of old magazines, for it seems that everywhere we go, a *Harrowsmith* reader has been there before us. It's a magazine for back-to-the-landers, with articles on bee-keeping and gardening, with advertisements for tractors and wind generators and water purifiers.

We find copies of *Harrowsmith* piled in the corners of abandoned homes, brick-like chunks of them on the edge of clearings, yellowed pages plastered like billboards to hand-hewn planks. And we know, at some time, someone has sat there by a kerosene lamp drooling over the little classified ads for "Troy Bilt Roto-Tillers" and "Forty-Two Easy Paté Recipes."

They've been set carefully aside, never used to light a fire in the stove or sop the dampness from water-filled boots. They've been read, and dreamed over, and read again. And the sad thing is that they're always left behind, along with the canning-jar lids and the tobacco tins filled with pretzel-shaped nails.

From the boat shed, we went south, and sheltered from hurricane-force winds in a place called Rock Inlet. The wharfinger at nearby Namu was surprised we'd entered it. He stood on the dock and stared at us, rocking on his heels. No one ever goes into Rock Inlet, he said.

He was an elderly man, officious looking, with a ledger tucked under his arm. "I say, old bean," he said, rocking forward, then back. "It seems to me it's called Rock Inlet for a reason."

We'd found out why, bouncing off an underwater boulder with the engine shuddering in reverse. But we'd found old floats in there to lie against, and a trailer that had been a camp of some sort.

And, under the bunk and piled by date, a collection of *Harrowsmiths*.

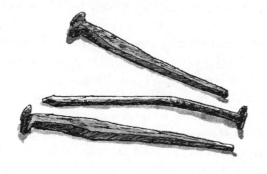

Bar Hopping

THEY ARE GONE—ALL SAVE THREE. They came in a box, in a big cardboard chest bound tightly with tape. There was a message from my brother: "Open after leaving dock." We wedged the box up in the bow, and we could hear them inside it as the boat rocked, hear them slithering and rustling, squirming in there.

For three days we looked at the box, tapped at the box, pried at its corners. And on the day we left, before we'd gone as far as Fairview, we broke out the box and hauled it up to the cockpit. I slit through the tape, cracked open the lid. Kristin peered over my shoulder.

"Oh my," she said. "Oh my."

They were chocolate bars. One hundred and ten chocolate bars. On most of them were messages, the wrappers turned inside out to carry wishes for a safe voyage and greetings in English and Spanish and Greek. We sorted through them like pirates through a chest of foreign coins—guineas, doubloons, and Louis-d'ors—chortling as they slid through our fingers.

"I hope your trip would be exciting one. I wish you good wind and good luck. Vladi."

"Stay away from the Triangle!"

"Qué tal? Permindar."

"You missed the most awesome meal. Chef Tom."

They were messages from Banff, written nearly four months before, when my brother was teaching at the Banff School of Fine Arts. He'd collected the chocolate bars that the students and artists habitually bought with their leftover food allowance.

A sculptor brazed a spidery web of brass rods into a Mr. Big holder. Photographers wrapped their Aero bars in weird photographs. A poet wrote:

> Oh baby blow wind into my
> sails make me billow
> and you shall see me
> froth like the very sea.

"Let's eat the boring ones first," said Kristin. And day by day, in harbours down the coast, we worked through the box, saving for last the clever bars and the funny ones.

Off Cape Caution, she opened a Fruit-and-Nut bar. "No message on here,"

she said, and out fell a strip of heavy paper with four tiny pictures taped in a row. It was "Dreaming, a very short film," and it starred a beautiful woman with a candle and a flimsy nightgown.

I tacked that one to the bulkhead. "It's art," I told her.

Anchored in Harlequin Bay, I opened another Fruit-and-Nut bar and found part two of the film. The girl was naked now, except for a tiny jeweled case that she held in her lap. The next evening in Hardy Bay, Kristin looked in the box and said, "Oh. Someone's gone through here and opened all the Fruit-and-Nut bars."

On the last day of the trip, I ate the Aero bar with its picture of shark fins swimming on the wrapper. "In case of emergency," it said. "Throw in water."

Now, as I said, only three are left. They are a set, tied with elastic. There's a Lust Bar, "to be consumed in the heat of the moment," and a Poetry Bar, "for a moment of inspiration." At the bottom is a Silly Bar.

"When are we going to eat the silly bar?" asks Kristin.

I show her the words on the wrapper: "To be consumed when lust and poetry vanish."

The Flight of the Skipper

THE SKIPPER WAS A PROBLEM. I was flying south to meet Kristin, to fetch our new boat from Seattle. I could send tools and charts to my parents in Ladysmith; I could carry the clothes and cameras and lifejackets. But the problem was the Skipper.

"She's a dog," said Kristin. "Just put her in a kennel."

"A kennel?!" I said.

"It's the kindest thing." The Skipper had never flown before. She would be lonely and scared. I would have to carry her through the airport, through customs, through Seattle in the rush hour. "She'd be in a cage," said Kristin. "She'd hate that."

"You might be right," I said. So I drove out to the kennel with the Skipper perched on the seat beside me. I would just have a look, I thought. The Skipper stared out the window, laughing, like a doddering old woman not

knowing she was going to visit the rest home. And I asked them at the kennel if I could bring food for the Skipper.

"Sure," they said. "We have a fridge. If she's on a special diet—on medication—we can . . . "

"No," I said, "I mean like hot dogs."

It didn't seem so bad. I sent the charts to Ladysmith, and told my parents the Skipper would go to a kennel.

"A kennel?!" my father said. "Oh, the poor thing. The poor wee thing."

"She'll like it," I said. "She'll have an outdoor run, like a patio, and it's right beside the sea and she can sit there and stare at the ocean and watch for otters and remember her days on the sailboat."

"And wonder," said my father, "if those days are behind her."

It was too heartbreaking. I phoned Kristin again. I said, "I'm bringing her down."

The vet gave me valium. I fed it to the Skipper, chopped up and hidden in bits of hot dog. I crammed her into the cage and slammed shut the door. It was close. I nearly snagged my finger on her teeth.

She rode in the baggage compartment, in the dark and the cold, unheated at thirty thousand feet. I could hear her barking during take-off, and she never stopped. The plane went howling and whining south for six hundred miles.

I found her crying at the carousel, yapping like a coyote. I put her on a baggage cart and headed off. And people kept stopping, coming to look, bending down to peer inside the cage, risking their fingers and noses to see what strange and exotic animal was being carted through the international gate.

"She's angry," I said. "She's in a bad mood," I said. "That's the Skipper." I felt like the orderly in "Silence of the Lambs," wheeling Hannibal Lecter on his dolly.

She barked through immigration and barked through customs. She barked for forty minutes in a turbo-prop to Seattle. And somewhere over Bellevue, the lady beside me called for the stewardess.

"Is there a dog on this plane?" she asked.

"Yes," said the stewardess. "Way in the back."

I told her it was my dog. "That's the Skipper," I said.

The lady smiled. "It's so nice," she said, "when someone travels with his pet."

A Tale of Two Sisters

WHEN THEY WERE BUILT, you couldn't tell one from the other. They were sisters, whaleboat sisters made of wood and copper and bronze—from gunwale to keel the same in every way, right down to their matched mooring cleats.

They hung in davits, head to toe, on the deck of a U.S. mine sweeper. And for twenty years they travelled that way, like possum babies on the back of their mother. From her east-coast base she might have steamed south on the Cuban blockade, face-to-face with Soviet missile ships; sailed in NATO fleets, guarded seaways. And at some point she might have moved to the Pacific, perhaps to Southeast Asia, taking the whaleboats to the war in Vietnam.

And when twenty years passed, the mother ship was torn apart for scrap. By then the whaleboat sisters were old and battered; ribs were cracked, planks were missing altogether. A huge crane plucked them from the mine sweeper's deck, and lowered them into the rubble of the shipyard.

They would have been crushed and burned if not for two young men who dreamed of sailing. They bought the boats, repaired them and painted them, fitted them with keels and masts. It was a new life for the sisters; one was given the Greek name *Archae,* meaning "beginning," the other was named in French: *Nid,* for nest. And they went away with their men, on their separate ways.

The sisters grew older; they changed owners, and changed again. They were thirty-three years old when I bought *Nid,* knowing nothing of *Archae.* I

was told by people in lonely places of a boat—"just like yours"—that was selling fresh-made bread to the cruisers in Desolation Sound. And for a week or two in the summer, we were just a few miles apart, only an island between us, but it seemed the sisters would never meet again.

In Port Hardy the owners of *Archae* found a book with a picture of *Nid* and headed north to find *Archae's* sister. They were a wonderful couple. He was a professional chef who baked bread at Desolation Sound; she was Australian, and filled the log with stories of their travels. They hoisted tanbark sails— mizzen and main and topsail—and tacked into headwinds and tides. They had three hundred miles to go to find *Nid*, and would sail all the way.

In a narrow passage connecting nothing to nowhere, *Archae* met a man in a speedboat. The whaleboat looked familiar to the man; he thought at first it was *Nid*. The speedboat's skipper had met me only once, had brought me a bucket of shrimp for a solitary feast in a mountainous anchorage. He told the couple about that encounter, and how they could find me on the sister of *Archae*.

But a few days earlier, about the time her sister left Port Hardy, I'd sold *Nid* to somebody else.

Archae came north. She anchored in the same places *Nid* had the summer before. It was as though she had picked up the scent of her sister, and followed it from bay to bay, her anchor gouging out the same bits of seafloor, her shadow falling on the same rocks and trees. She tacked up Principe and Petrel Channel, past Oona River and Holland Rock. She passed within half a mile of *Nid* before she anchored at Cow Bay, and the couple went to town.

Within hours, the new owners of *Nid* set off from Dodge Cove, where she'd been sold. They were going on a cruise that would take them miles from *Archae*. But first they went to town, and, by chance, to Cow Bay.

They tied up to an elegant, black-hulled boat. They took a line from their mooring cleat and passed it around another that was exactly the same.

And the sisters sat side by side, for the first time in twenty years, reunited.

The Seven-year Summer

TODAY I SOLD MY BOAT. The whole process was long and drawn out, but in the end it was sudden. When the tide went out she was mine, and when it came back in, she was not.

I had one more job to do, one more trip. And when the tide was high I went down to move her from the grid to the dock.

It was late at night. The cove was quiet and calm. My little *Nid* sat nearly on the shore, where she'd waited all day leaning against the pilings. When I climbed down to the deck she didn't move as she normally would, like a dog waking for an expected walk. The keel was still on the bottom.

I opened the hatch, and crawled inside.

How many times had I done that over the last seven years? Five thousand; ten thousand? Probably more. I started the engine, then sat in the cockpit and watched the tide rise over the rudder, over planks and seams. When it reached the waterline I said, "Let's go," and she lifted up, coming awake, and shook herself with a tremble.

It wasn't a long trip. In half an hour I was home again, and the house was dark. I took out the logbooks, the journals of our trips, and read them all at once, the dates running together into a single summer seven years long.

June 12: It never gets completely dark. We reef down for the night, change from the big jib to the smaller staysail while the wind is still quite strong. At

dawn we're halfway down Laredo Channel, steering by the lights and the loom of the land against the sky.

June 13: Off Ivory, in the growing dusk, a Minke whale latches onto us and follows a long way, circling the boat.

June 22: Replenished water supplies from a small creek where we saw a deer drinking in early morning.

June 26: Escorted part of the way down Mathieson Channel by a school of porpoises. Weather miserable—cold, windy and squally.

July 1: Anchored in the bay of floating rocks.

August 3: A particularly friendly, little brown porpoise stays with us for miles, swimming up under the rudder and turning on his back to gaze up at us. Try feeding him sardines, but not much interest.

August 21: The moon, still far from full, has risen over the trees behind us. The sky is flickering with northern lights. All around the boat, things are splashing and rippling at the water. Far away, a wolf is howling.

August 23: A giant sea lion has taken residence in the bay. He surfaces very close alongside, giving the Skipper an awful fright. We put her on her leash, unsure of the eating habits of sea lions.

August 25: By afternoon the wind is in the mid-30s, gusting over 40 knots. Even in the short fetch of the anchorage, quite a sea is building, and *Nid* heels sharply to the gusts, then settles back on the anchors. Rain is persistent. Out in the channel, the sea is white.

August 30: Late evening, we motor across the channel to Dodge Cove, the sun bright in our faces. Tie up and slide shut the hatches. We're home from the sea.

I closed the logbooks and put them away. It surprised me to feel so terribly sad. But I would never again sail on the *Nid*—or sail *with* her, for that was the way that it seemed. We would never again set off for a place we didn't know; never again come home. I thought of her sitting quietly empty, stripped of all that was mine. And I felt sorry for her, all by herself, down there at the dock.

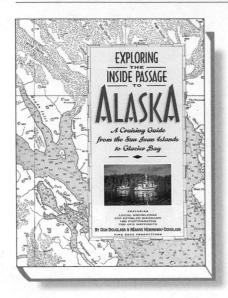

EXPLORING THE INSIDE PASSAGE TO ALASKA

A Cruising Guide from the San Juan Islands to Glacier Bay

By Don Douglass & Réanne Hemingway-Douglass

"On our next trip . . . your pilothouse guide will be the first book on board."
—Jane Lehmer, Seattle

The Inside Passage to Alaska offers one of the world's best cruising grounds for small craft. Almost completely protected, these waters give access to a pristine wilderness of breathtaking beauty—thousands of islands, deeply-cut fjords, tidewater glaciers and icebergs. The Douglasses who cruise to and from Alaska every year supply skippers with all the up-to-date local knowledge they need. Suggested itineraries for two-week to three-month voyages from Puget Sound to Glacier Bay include the West Coast Outer Passage, a remote, smooth-water route from Glacier Bay south.

Featuring: • Expert Local Knowledge • 250 detailed anchor diagrams • 180 photographs 700 GPS Waypoints • Large Format • ISBN 0-938665-33-2 • 400 pages

EXPLORING VANCOUVER ISLAND'S WEST COAST

A Cruising Guide

By Don Douglass

Nowhere does the tourist motto *Super, Natural British Columbia!* come more alive than on the West Coast of Vancouver Island. With five great sounds, sixteen major inlets, and an abundance of spectacular wildlife, the largest island on the west coast of North America is a cruising paradise. The Douglasses consider their voyages along Vancouver Island's West Coast some of their most satisfying adventures. In this guide they give small craft skippers the kind of local knowledge they need to circumnavigate the island and drop hook in more than 150 intimate coves.

Featuring: Expert Local Knowledge • 150 detailed anchor diagrams • 75 photographs 250 GPS Waypoints • Large Format • ISBN 0-938665-26-X • 288 pages

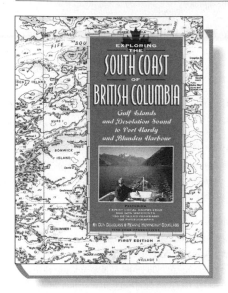

EXPLORING THE SOUTH COAST OF BRITISH COLUMBIA

Gulf Islands and Desolation Sound to Port Hardy and Blunden Harbour

By Don Douglass & Réanne Hemingway-Douglass

"Clearly the most thorough, best produced and most useful [guides] available . . . particularly well thought out and painstakingly researched."
— *NW Yachting*

"Emphasizes local knowledge to 'fill in the blanks.'" — *Pacific Yachting*

Exploring the South Coast of British Columbia is designed by experts to give small boat skippers the kind of accurate, up-to-date information they need to set sail for the unmatched natural beauty of the Pacific Northwest. Its complete descriptions of routes, and anchorages are based on the authors' personal experience of each location and on information from local skippers not available anywhere else.

Featuring: • Expert Local Knowledge • 150 detailed anchor diagrams • 175 photographs 600 GPS Waypoints • Large Format • ISBN 0-938665-44-8 • 304 pages

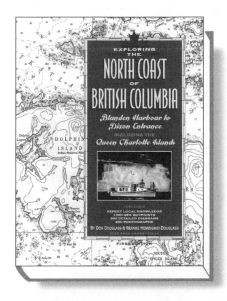

EXPLORING THE NORTH COAST OF BRITISH COLUMBIA

Blunden Harbour to Dixon Entrance Including the Queen Charlotte Islands

"The book is stunning. Nobody has given the cruising community what this book gives."
— R. Hale, author, *Waggoner*

Exploring the North Coast of British Columbia takes sea-faring explorers from the famous Nakwakto Rapids to the Alaska border. This ultimate pilothouse resource describes previously uncharted Spiller Channel and Griffin Passage, the stunning scenery of Nakwakto Rapids and Seymour Inlet, Fish Egg Inlet, Queens Sound, and Hakai Recreation Area. It helps you plot a course for the beautiful South Moresby Island of the Queen Charlottes, known for its rare flora and fauna, and for its historical sites of native Haida culture.

Featuring: • Expert Local Knowledge • 250 detailed anchor diagrams • 250 photographs 1500 GPS Waypoints • Large Format • ISBN 0-938665-45-6 • 432 pages

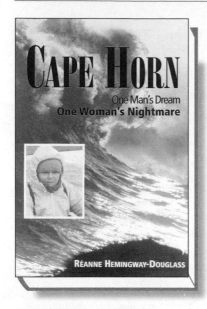